Advance Praise for Pro-Active Parent Coaching

Greg has responded once again to speak into a great need in society. Already a proven child leadership coaching specialist, Greg now addresses a most paramount aspect of human society - the responsibility of parenting well! His underlying premise is captured in the subtitle of this book, "Capturing the Heart of Your Child". Parents must set a priority to positively impact 'their' child's heart in spite of the many pulls and pressures of contemporary society. This need is underscored in the book of Proverbs (2:10) "For wisdom will enter your HEART, and knowledge will be pleasant to your soul."(NIV)

"Pro-Active Parent Coaching: Capturing the Heart of Your Child" will be an incredibly valuable source of relevant stories, wise biblical principles, relational suggestions and stimulating assignments, all of which will assist you as a parent to capture and impact the heart of your child. Your journey with this book will assist greatly as you make the truth in Psalm 37:31 a reality, "The law of their God is in their hearts; their feet do not slip." May your child's heart be yours and may you be well grounded in his/her heart! Enjoy the rewarding expedition!

     Rev. Douglas Moore, District Superintendent, Pentecostal Assemblies of Canada
         (Maritime District)

Having the privilege of spending time with Greg, Lynn and their children and knowing them well, I have seen the principles of Pro-Active Parent Coaching at work first hand in their family. Through everyday life, to major decisions faced together, the practices of Pro-Active Parent Coaching are fundamental to the healthy dynamic they enjoy. Greg's passion for healthy relationships within the family is the heartbeat behind his practical approach and real life examples. I highly recommend 'Pro-Active Parent Coaching: Capturing the Heart of Your Child' for parents of all ages who desire to have a close and lasting relationship with their children; Who want to be an active part of seeing their children/youth, journey into responsible adulthood and embrace the destiny God has for them.

     Sarabeth Strathdee, Children's & Youth Pastor

Greg provides tremendous insight to the fact that children are not seeking independence from their parents' as we sometimes think, but rather from our limiting parenting style! This is a significant breakthrough concept for parenting. Greg's practical advice makes connecting with your child realistic and attainable. This book is backed with biblical insights that will save and strengthen your relationship. A must read for all parents no matter the age of your child.

     Nick & Michelle Allaire, 2 children aged 7 & 12

I believe that this is a much-needed book that can be used by parents to help their children discover their unique calling and gifts. It seeks to develop and cultivate change where it must begin – in the heart of the child, no matter what age they may be. It reminds us that God is at work in our children and has given us the great privilege of working with him to help our children discover a life of significance and purpose.

     Mitchell Foley, Pastor Atlantic Baptist Convention, 2 children aged 4 & 10

This is a marvellous tool for parents that I wish I had read when my children were young. As a mother of two adult sons, and with a background in social work/psychology, I had come some ways toward this approach to parenting (as opposed to the child-rearing practices of my parents' generation), but I could certainly have benefitted from the clear guidelines Greg gives us in the coaching model. I feel this will be a blessing to any family where these principles are applied!

Lynn Quinn, BSW, 2 adult children

I feel very privileged to be part of the process of seeing this book come to life. As I have read and reread the concepts of this book, I can't help but be changed in my attitudes and awareness of how I am interacting and responding to my own teenaged child. It is a gift from God that is right now helping to shape our conversations in the midst of some very serious, life altering decisions. I am realizing how crucial my supportive questions are to the health and direction of my daughter's choices and actions. It's not the easiest course I have taken, but it is by far the most effective.

Connie delaMorandiere, 3 children, 1 teen and 2 adults

Note from the Author

The thought of marriage itself invoked fear within my heart, let alone parenting. Although I experienced the care and love of a mother growing up, I did not have a strong male influence within my life, and couldn't imagine what I should do as a husband or a dad.

It was after I made a commitment to Christ at 19 years of age, that I began to realize my history wasn't a handicap, and I had the greatest example of parenthood anyone could ask for, God Himself.

Through my study of Scripture, observing how God relates to us as His children, and my growing experience with Him, I began to understand what an Empowering Parenting Style looked like. There is a wonderful blend of love and acceptance, with a willingness to allow growth in responsibility through experience and pain. Along with this growing knowledge of God, came a confidence that I could commit to marriage, be a good husband, and parent too.

As a result of this growing confidence, I risked asking Lynn to marry me, and, she agreed. After 17 years of marriage we have three wonderful children, Katelyn, Hannah, and Joshua, who have helped bring life to the Pro-Active Parent Coaching model you are about to experience. We have 'practiced' coaching principles throughout our ministry and implemented coaching very early within our children's lives, which has been very well received.

Over the course of many conversations with Tony, he has consistently challenged us to formalize our parent coaching model, which is now complete and we are excited to share it with you.

If there is one thing we hope for as you read through and experience our journey, it would be this: that you too would be inspired by what God can do in and through you and your family, as you emulate His approach to parent coaching.

About the Author

Greg is an ordained minister within the Pentecostal Assemblies of Canada, a certified Birkman Method® Consultant, and has received his coach training through Tony Stoltzfus of Coach22. Greg has actively served in ministry for over 20 years, in various ministry roles ranging from children's & youth ministry, assistant pastor, church planting, sectional presbyter, and most recently, serving as an 'interim' pastor for churches in transition. His experience in pastoral ministry, volunteering in primary and secondary schools, and parenting his own three children, has given Greg a passion for healthy relationships within families today.

Pro-Active Parent Coaching
Capturing the Heart of Your Child

A Parent's Guide to Coaching by Gregory Bland

Cover Design by Naomi Brock
www.naomibrock.com

Images used in this book created and designed by Gregory Bland

To order copies of this book,
or for more information on
Pro-Active Parent Coaching
and our training options, visit
www.pro-activeparentcoaching.com

Contents

Acknowledgements

My deepest appreciation goes to God without whose work in my life I would never have become a parent, let alone, write a book about parent coaching. This is for You, as a testimony to the positive change You can bring in a life, a home and a family.

My biggest thank you goes to Lynn, my wonderful wife, Katelyn, Hannah and Joshua, our three children, who continue to offer support and encouragement throughout this project. Without them, Pro-Active Parent Coaching would simply be theory, instead they have brought it to life.

Appreciation goes to everyone who has helped throughout this process and especially to:

Tony Stoltzfus, my friend and coach who walked through this transitional journey with our family. He provided us with the necessary support, encouragement, and accountability that we needed as we continued moving forward with this project. It is highly probable that I would not have written this book, had God not brought Tony into my life through the coach training initiative of our fellowship. I could not have written this book without the time spent in coach training with Tony, or having him draw out of me what God had already deposited within our hearts about parenting and parent coaching. Much of the content of this book reflects our heart as parents and the coaching principles learned from Tony that we have adapted to our own work with parents.

Sarabeth Strathdee, a close family friend and partner in ministry for over 10 years. She has read more draft copies of this book than anyone should have to. The time she has offered to us, in reading, proofing and bouncing ideas off of has been incredible. Without your involvement, *Pro-Active Parent Coaching: Capturing the Heart of Your Child* would not be what it is today. A huge thank you goes to Sarabeth, for the time she has invested in this project, and the constant encouragement she has offered our family, as we brought Pro-Active Parent Coaching to life.

The family of Cornerstone Community Church, who in their selflessness recognized and affirmed God's call upon our lives, and released us from our pastoral responsibilities, to pursue this dream. Although now separated by many miles, you will remain forever in our hearts for the support and encouragement you continue to offer us.

The attendees of our first *Pro-Active Parent Coaching* training course. Your involvement, feedback, and enthusiasm, helped solidify within our minds the direction God was asking us to move toward. Thank you for allowing us to experiment with you.

All the children, teens and young adults who gave me permission to 'experiment' upon you with coaching and record our sessions for training purposes. You remain an integral part of Pro-Active Parent Coaching. Together we will make a difference within the hearts and lives of many families who will embrace and implement Pro-Active Parent Coaching within their own lives.

Everyone else who has provided encouragement throughout this writing project. Your support was often the fuel I needed to continue moving forward. Thank you.

Foreword

Taking the risk to decide together as a family on a new church was a turning point in our family life. My wife and I felt God was saying that our next season of church involvement was going to be about the kids, and that we needed to find a place that worked for them whether or not it did for us. Since their growth was the focus, we stuck our necks out and decided to believe God could speak to all four of us about where we should go.

"We're going to visit several different churches, pray about each one, and I believe that God will speak to both of you as well as mom and I about what the right choice is," I announced in a family meeting. "What else do you want to know about this?"

As usual, our vocal ten-year-old had a bunch of questions. "Where will we visit? How will we know which one is right? What will we get to do there?" As we patiently explained the process, our eight-year-old son sat quietly, a sober look on his face as he took it all in. He didn't have any questions, and we weren't quite sure what was going on in his head that evening.

The choice came down to two churches. One had a solid youth program with good leadership and a healthy congregation, and kept the kids in the sanctuary to experience worship up until the sermon time. The second one had candy, soda, puppet shows and videos for the kids while the adults were in worship.

That's when I started to get a little nervous about my discernment plan. Were they really going to hear God speak, or would they just pick the place with the candy and movies? My wife and I were leaning pretty strongly toward the first congregation—what would we do if we had a split decision? And how would I deal with telling them God would speak to them if they didn't hear anything.

After our second visit to the final church, we had another family meeting in the car on the way home. I started by asking our ten-year-old what she was sensing. She announced that the "spiritual atmosphere" was better in the first church, and she thought we should go there. Our quiet eight-year-old said he liked the candy, but that he didn't learn anything there, so he thought we should go to the place where he could learn more about God. My wife and I were blown away: God really had spoken to our kids, and we were all in agreement

That launched a family pattern of hearing God together on important decisions. Seven years later, Kathy and I began to feel a stirring to relocate– while our kids were still in High School. We submitted the decision to the family like usual, and found that God had already spoken to them: in spite of their connections and school and with friends, they were ready to move all the way across the country. The place we ended up going to was in our daughter's heart first. I never would have thought of coming to the place that will probably result in fulfilling my life call if I hadn't been listening to God speak through my children.

I've been looking forward to the publishing of this book for years (and actively prodded Greg to write it!), because I believe the application of coaching to parenting will lead to an enormous breakthrough in our ability to raise world-changing sons and daughters. We know how to care for babies; we know how to mentor and instruct young children, but so often parents are at a total loss for what to do with their teens. We're aware we should be preparing them to live on their own as adults, but there is nothing in our parenting toolkit that seems to fit the task. Coaching fills that void, because it gives us practical handles on how to give kids responsibility (which is the only way they'll really learn to handle it) while still influencing them.

The cry of many a teenager's heart is to be heard, to be believed in, to be trusted. This book shows you how to do that. The anguish of many parents' hearts is feeling like their kids are becoming more and more distant, and not knowing how to bridge the gap. This book shows you how to love them in a way that they want to receive, while at the same time helping them be more responsible and not less. I don't know a better way to build a truly interdependent relationship with those you parent.

Greg has taken coaching concepts that I stumbled around implementing in my own family and gone much farther with them than I ever could. And after coaching him for several years, I can vouch that this comes out of his life. I am amazed by the faith journey his family is on, and by how he and Lynn have empowered their kids in the midst of it.

By offering a simple coaching model and beautifully illustrating how to use it with real-life dialogs, this book makes parent coaching something anyone can do. It works with kids of any age—in fact, starting early like we did in our home is the best way to implement it.

But while the concepts here are simple, changing the way you parent isn't always easy. Something as rudimentary as asking open questions may require changing the conversational habits of a lifetime. As you try to honor your kids desires and hear their hearts, it will probably bring some of your own junk to the surface.

That's hard work. But the payoff is enormous. The same relational approach that makes your kids feel honored and believed in will do the same for your husband, your wife, your friends, your coworkers—everyone you know.

Coaching at its heart is a disciplined way of communicating that you believe in people. It's faith that God is already present, already speaking, already at work in the ones you love. I believed my kids could hear the voice of God, and they rose to it—and eventually their ability to hear had a big influence on my journey. Believing in them and sharing responsibility made them peers and not just kids. That's a relationship we'll enjoy for the rest of our lives.

I believe Jesus' church can be the world leaders in bringing coaching to the parenting arena. We can be the model everyone turns to for consistently producing healthy, secure, interdependent kids who still love to hang out with their parents even when they're in High School. And I believe this book can be a big part of making that happen.

Tony Stoltzfus
Master Coach Trainer, author of Leadership Coaching and Coaching Questions

Chapter 1

"Connecting with our children may not be as complicated as one might initially think."

Coaching: A Natural Approach to Parenting

The tones of rushing water deepened as the sink filled to capacity. I stood gazing through the steam covered window across the yard as the snow fell gently upon the ground. "Katelyn, are you ready? It's our turn to do the dishes this evening!," I called as I reached for the dishcloth. Katelyn quickly came and stood beside me as we embarked upon the noble task of washing, drying and putting away the evening dinner dishes.

Connecting with our children is not as complicated as one might initially think. Simply meeting our children at their greatest point of interest is an easy, effective and powerful way to connect.

> By way of example, continue reading the coaching conversation between our 10-year-old daughter and myself which transformed a mundane activity into a memorable moment of heart connection between us. As you continue reading this coaching conversation watch for:
>
> - What creates openness in conversation between us resulting in a genuine connection?
> - Significant shifts that take place within the conversation.
> - Patterns that you see emerging within the coaching conversation itself.

Moving from the Mundane to the Memorable

A dish rattling in the sink after dinner almost always indicates a mundane household chore is underway, but this evening that perspective changed dramatically when these noises were interrupted by a significant and powerful question from Katelyn.

Coaching Conversation

"Dad, when you were younger, what did you want out of life?"

Pleasantly surprised by this question, I turned, looked in her eyes and affirmed, *"That's a very good question, honey!"* then continued, *"You already have a good head start on me as a young person."*

"In what way?"

"Well, for starters, I didn't have a Mom and Dad at home while I was growing up, I lived with your Nana but not your Grandpa. Unlike you, Katelyn, God wasn't a part of our lives and I didn't have a church family either. So at the time I didn't realize that life had any significant meaning or purpose to it. Never giving much thought about life beyond the present, I just kind of lived for myself in the moment. What felt right and good, what I wanted and desired; well, those are the kinds of things that I thought about and chased after."

"Like what Daddy?"

"Friends were a big deal to me, and having their acceptance and approval was very important. As I look back on my teen years though, I recognize that I wasn't a great friend to others. Still, I did have one thing going for me though - a very strong work ethic."

"What's a 'strong work ethic'?

"Well, that means I was a very hard worker."

"Ohh, ok."

"This helped me get and keep jobs as a young teen, which then gave me a taste for what money could do for me. Money gave me a great sense of security and freedom that I hadn't felt before. I bought a lot of my own stuff, and was quite proud of that. I bought my first car when I was 15, that way I'd have it when I turned 16 and got my license. I also bought my own street motorcycle when I was 16. I remember one big purchase that I made which my Mom really didn't approve of."

"What was that?"

"Another car, a Camaro Z28. Actually, before I bought it I asked her if she would mind. There was a part of me that wanted to honor her because I lived with her. But she did not want me to buy

Observation

I connect with Katelyn here by meeting her at her greatest point of interest; what I wanted out of life when I was younger. By continuing this conversation, I not only connect with her in this moment, but affirm that I am open to her asking such questions.

Throughout this conversation I model transparency, an important characteristic that fosters openness within relationships.

Conversational Pattern: *Connecting, Asking, Listening, and Clarifying* to ensure understanding.

Notice, Katelyn's questions are aroused by her curiosity about my life when I was younger. She simply draws more information out of me by asking simple open questions such as, 'Like what?' 'What was that?' 'Tell me more.'

that car and let me know that she did not want it parked in her driveway. That is where our relationship was hurt, not because she said no, but because I went ahead and bought it anyway. We're fine now as you know, but for a while, our relationship was pretty rough. Buying that car also meant I had to go in debt to purchase it, so I had to work very, very hard to keep up with the payments and that was tough as a teenager in school. But you know what, that wasn't the worst decision I made as a young teen."

"No?"

"Nope, the worst decision I made led me into an addiction to alcohol when I was just a couple of years older than you are now. In my mind I thought, 'It's my life, my body, my decision, it's no one else's business what I do!' I didn't give any thought at all to the fact that my decisions affect others around me."

Katelyn listened with interest as she slowly dried each dish and placed it carefully in its proper place within the kitchen cabinet. She paused for a moment, then turned and looked at me as a wry smile broke upon her face. Curiously I asked, *"What are you thinking right now?"*

She sheepishly looked at me, and responded with a giggle, "So, are you saying that you were selfish?"

Laughing, I reached for the next dish, affirmed her intuition and replied, *"Yes, young lady, if you boiled it all down, that is exactly what I am saying. It was all about me!"*

She laughed as she said, "Tell me more, Daddy."

"Well, honey, I am thankful that this is not the end of the story. You see, there was a significant event that took place when I was 18, which changed my thinking, and ultimately the direction of my life. One evening, while at a dance club, I had an interesting experience through which I knew God was trying to get my attention and have me think differently about Him and my life. In that moment, I recognized that many around me, including myself, were not really as happy as we pretended we were. That night I did a very important thing, I left the dance club and prayed, 'God, if you are real and you want me, reveal yourself to me!'" And He did, He answered that

My transparency continues to set the stage for Katelyn to open up.

prayer, but He didn't do it with a flash of light or something extraordinary. He did it in the most common way. He revealed Himself to me through other people, and you know what, I think He did that to show me that our lives do affect other people. Anyway, up to this point one young man had been asking me over and over to go to his youth ministry outings but I continually refused him. True to his character, the following week he asked me again. This time though, I accepted the invitation and went with him. I found myself there, with 30 other teenagers, having a great time, but with one major difference."

"What was that?"

"There was no alcohol."

"Cool."

"Yeah, it was cool. My curiosity about all of this was strong enough that I began attending this youth ministry and the church all the time. I actually developed a pretty good relationship with the youth pastor and many others in the church. For several months I hung with two crowds, the church family, and my dance club buddies. But, I began to realize that I was really living two lives and would have to make a decision, either serve God or turn my back on Him."

"At first, I chose the night clubs, but one evening, just after my 19th birthday I finally gave in to God. That was a huge thing for me and I learned a very valuable lesson about God that night."

"What was that?"

"Well, right then, I was kneeling at our toilet throwing up. I know it's not a real pretty picture, but I learned that God meets us wherever we are when we call out to Him."

"Wow."

"Yeah, that also showed me something else; He accepts us for who we are, and doesn't expect us to be all cleaned up first. You know, that night God took my addiction away and I haven't had a drop of alcohol from that moment to this. I knew without question that God accepted me and embraced me as one of His own. And I can honestly say that my whole outlook on life changed."

"In what way did it change?"

"Well, over time I began to understand that there

was meaning to life and it was a whole lot more than simply buying stuff for me. I also recognized that our lives have an incredible influence upon others which will last way beyond this life, and I wanted that influence to be a positive one. God also helped me to understand and overcome my fear that all marriages would end in divorce. Because of this I risked asking your Mom to marry me and, of course, you know she said, 'Yes!' In time, God gave us three children who Mommy and Daddy love very, very much and He continues to lead us in helping other people by having us pastor a great church family here in Lively."

Katelyn listened intently as I shared. Taking it all in, she remained silent for a few moments then thoughtfully asked, "Daddy, what do you think I should do with my life?"

Katelyn's question marks a significant shift in conversation. Up to this point the focus has been upon understanding Daddy more, she now changes the focus toward herself.

Reflection

Before moving forward with this parent coaching conversation, take a moment to reflect on Katelyn's question, *"Daddy, what do you think I should do with my life?"* This is an incredible question to be asked as a parent. Think about what you might say and do if you were asked the same question by your child.

- What are the first thoughts that come to your mind?
- How would you approach this question from your child?
- What would you say?

Take a moment longer and step into their shoes. You are a sincere child who has risked opening up and asking this important question to your parent(s). "Mom/Dad, what do you think I should do with my life?"

Describe how you would like your parents to respond:

- What is their body language telling you?
- What are they specifically saying?
- What attitudes and values are their words communicating?
- Capture the moment, live it. What is this doing within you? What feelings, thoughts or emotions are you experiencing?
- As your parents speak to you how are their words and actions influencing your thoughts and attitude toward them?

Remember, what you desire from your parents in that moment, may be the very thing your child needs from you right now.

Coaching Conversation

"That is a very important question to consider, Katelyn," I affirmed. *"Before we jump into what you should do with your life, can I share another thought that might help you out a bit?"*

"Sure."

"In my understanding, God is more concerned with who we are becoming and our character, than He is with what we are doing. I think it is very important that we pay close attention to what He is doing within us; the character that He is forming through the things we experience; the gifts and talents that He has given to us; and the unique call that He places upon our lives. See, God is constantly forming and shaping us because what we do will flow naturally from who He is creating us to be. Katelyn, your life will naturally have an impact upon others, and if you're a young woman with great character, that impact will not only be long lasting, but positive too. As God continues to mold and shape you into the young lady He desires you to be, my guess is, He will present you with several options about what you can do with your life. Any of these options will be acceptable to Him and will fit well with who He has made you to be."

Pausing for a few moments here, I simply let silence fall, allowing her to consider, without distraction, the words that were spoken. After some time had passed, I continued by asking, *"Consider this, Katelyn; what have you noticed yourself thinking about a lot of the time?"*

After a few more moments of silence Katelyn opened up, "Well, I think a lot about the homeless, those who have no place to live, and no way to make money for food and stuff."

"Wow, that's interesting! Tell me more about this."

"Well, I would like to have a home with acreage, kind of like we have now, but a farm with a barn and horses, other animals and stuff like that. That way when I come across someone who doesn't have a home, they can come and live on the farm. They will be able to work with me, learn the skills and stuff they need to know so they can make it

Observation

Rather than simply take the opportunity to share what I want to, I honor Katelyn, by asking if I can share another thought with her. After Katelyn gives me permission to do so, I proceed sharing my thoughts..

Conversational Pattern: Silence is used frequently within a conversation after a significant statement or question to allow the child to fully consider without interruption what has been spoken.

on their own. When they are ready and able they could move out and get their own home and stuff like that. That is something I've thought a lot about and I think I'd really like to do something like this. What do you think, Daddy?"

Reflection

By engaging in this coaching conversation I was given an opportunity to catch a glimpse of Katelyn's heart. As her parents, Lynn and I had recognized compassion for others developing within her heart but quite frankly, we would never have guessed this was on her mind.

These five simple words, 'What do you think Daddy?' showed the trust that had developed between us and her willingness to be vulnerable by asking my opinion. In that moment I recognized the influential power she was giving to me and this presented me with an important decision. "How would I respond?"

Options:

A. I could take a typical adult response and dismiss this as the silly notion of a young child by simply brushing it off and changing the topic of conversation or shut her down with one of the following responses.

- "You know, kiddo, those are pretty lofty ideas for a child. Why don't you leave that big stuff for us adults to worry about?"
- "When you get your head out of the clouds and come back to reality, you will realize just how lofty that idea is."
- "Do you realize just how much money that would take?"
- "Do you honestly think God would place something that big within the heart of a 10-year-old?"
- "If that is something you really want to do, let me tell you what you need to do."

Or,

B. I could take the posture of a coach. Trusting that God is already at work within her heart and using this as an opportunity to support her growth in responsibility by, a. Refraining from simply telling her what I think. b. Engaging her in deeper thought and reflection by asking open non-leading questions. c. Authentically listening so that she may explore this dream further and discover what God may be doing within her. d. Supporting her growth in ability to discern what God may be doing within her.

A parent coach can open up more dialogue by responding with something like,

- "That's interesting, honey. Can you tell me more about that?"
- "That's incredible, maybe God is directing you in some way here. Can we explore this a bit more?"
- "What is it that excites you about that idea?"
- "Let's talk about this some more. Tell me what else you've been thinking?"

Coaching Conversation	Observation

"What do I think? Well, Honey, this really excites me. It also tells me a lot about what God is forming in your character. Your compassion and desire to help others is something that I respect and admire. That makes me proud to be your Daddy. Can I ask you some more questions about this 'dream'?"

"Yeah, that's OK."

"As you think about having a farm and helping the homeless in this way, what kind of feelings does that stir up within you?"

"I feel good! I know I would love helping other people in that way too. You know there are lots of people who need help like this. I think it would be great, helping them get the skills they need while working on the farm. I also like horses, farms and stuff, so I would be able to help others, while doing something that I like. That'd be cool too."

"That's true! As you think about helping others in that way, is there anything else that comes to mind?"

"I just like the idea of being able to help people. It makes me feel good inside when I do, and they appreciate it too. That means a lot to me."

"What else can you tell me about this dream of yours?"

Katelyn gladly continued, sharing details about what the farm would look like, her plan for involving the homeless in chores and gardening and what they could learn so they could live out on their own. She listed all the animals she wanted on the farm but most importantly for me, she let me know, "You can be there to help out too, Dad; I will need a good maintenance man."

As Katelyn shared her thoughts, I intentionally slowed the pace of washing dishes in order to give her plenty of time to put into words what was within her heart. As we concluded, I thanked her for sharing and affirmed, *"You know, Katelyn, God may very well have placed this dream in your heart. What could you do to explore this a bit more and discover what He is saying to you?"*

"Well, I could pray about it more."

"Definitely. Is there anything else that might

Coaching Pattern: I allow Katelyn to maintain control of the conversation by asking her permission to share thoughts/ideas, or ask further questions. This honors her as an individual and allows her to control the pace, direction, and depth of the conversation.

Coaching Pattern: *Asking* an open, non-leading question, then listening as they respond, brings more information out in the open. This helps us gain a true understanding of what they are thinking, feeling, and/or experiencing. It also prevents us from jumping to wrong conclusions.

Significant Shift in conversation. Up to this point I have been gathering information in order to understand what she has been thinking. I now transition from *understanding* to *supporting growth.*

Exploring Possibilities

help you understand what He is saying to you?"

"Umm, it may be a good idea to take some horse riding lessons too. That would help me know if I really like horses as much as I think I would."

"Those are both great possibilities. Is there anything else you can think of?"

- Reflective Pause -

"I could volunteer on a farm or at a Veterinary Clinic."

"Excellent, you're good at exploring possibilities. Is there one more thing you can think of?"

"No, I don't think so."

"OK, when you think of the possibilities you mentioned, praying, horse riding lessons, and volunteering, what would you like to do first?"

"I could begin praying about it tonight"

"Yes, you could, is that something you are committed to doing?"

"Yes, I am, I'll do that just before I go to bed."

"That's a great start, honey. How do you feel about your decision?"

"I am excited about it. Thanks, Dad, for talking with me about this."

"You're very welcome. I look forward to hearing what God says to you about this dream. When would you like to talk about it again?"

"Our date day next week would work."

"Sounds great. Is there any other way Daddy can help you right now?"

"No, it's all good."

"OK, as you talk with God about this, just know I am here if you need me. Even if it is before our date day, you just have to let me know."

"OK Dad, thank you."

Coaching Pattern: Continuing to ask, "Is there anything else?" helps our children move beyond the obvious and into a creative zone. Here is where she may begin considering new possibilities not considered before.

Assessing Desire: I want to know what she is personally motivated to work on.

Securing Commitment: I want to ensure that she is verbalizing a specific commitment to action.

This process naturally fosters further conversation where we can Encourage our child's Progress. I want to support and encourage Katelyn's discovery here, so I ask when we can talk about this again. This communicates my expectation that she will follow through, provides a healthy accountability structure, and affirms that I believe she can discern what God is saying to her.

Update

Three years have passed between the time Katelyn and I shared this coaching conversation together, and the completion of this chapter. It has been an amazing journey for Lynn and I as we have observed, and continued coaching Katelyn while she sorts out what God is doing within her. She has committed to further action with some of the other possibilities she generated that evening, which continues to develop her character and ability to navigate decisions and listen to God.

Katelyn has had the privilege of working through the pain of being considered too young to volunteer at a veterinary clinic, and wrestling with the reality of this dream when other adults challenged the 'reality' of it. Katelyn has become very proficient with horses, and during her lessons we recognized that she has a natural aptitude for working with horses.

Most recently we purchased a home next door to the horse farm where she received her first riding lessons. She set her heart upon volunteering there, when she approached them about this, they asked her if she would be interested in buying one of their horses. Her response was, "No, actually I would like to do a free lease. I will volunteer and do chores for you in exchange for the use of your horses." Their response was, "We can do that."

Arriving home that afternoon she excitedly shared the news with us. As a family we discussed and determined how much time Katelyn could reasonably spend at the farm and still maintain balance with schoolwork, relationships, recreation time, and household responsibilities. She then revisited the farm and made her proposal. Much to Katelyn's delight, they agreed with the schedule and the free lease was settled. As a result, Katelyn is gaining some incredible experience with farm work as she continues to discern what God is saying to her about this dream.

Sitting alone in the house one afternoon, fingers plinking away at the keyboard, my attention was momentarily pulled away by the ringing of our door bell. I walked quickly to the front door and was greeted with the following sight on our front lawn.

This is Katelyn, proudly taking our youngest, Joshua, for a ride on Robyn. What an incredible highlight this was in my day, as my mind flooded with the memories of our conversation three years prior, when all of this was just a dream.

As Katelyn continues to pursue this dream and discern what God is saying to her, Lynn and I offer the support, encouragement, and accountability she needs through coaching. We know all too well that soon she will be launching out on her own and these coachable moments are giving her a reservoir of experience from which she can draw wisdom as she navigates life outside of our home.

Pro-Active Parent Coaching is a natural approach to parenting that will strengthen relationships while providing our children with a healthy support structure for their growth and development.

Is parent coaching hard work at times? Definitely. Does it take commitment and self sacrifice? Absolutely. Is it worth the time and effort? Without question!

Chapter 2

"As a parent coach we play a significant role in supporting our child's dreams."

What is Pro-Active Parent Coaching?

Pro-Active Parent Coaching is a natural approach to parenting that will strengthen relationship while providing our children with a healthy support structure for their growth and development.

The *Pro-Active Parent Coaching* approach utilizes two conversational models, each with the specific purpose of supporting our children. The first model focuses upon *Supporting a Relationship through Understanding* by *Connecting, Asking, Listening and Clarifying.*

Understanding provides the relationship with the support it needs to naturally transition to the second stage of the model, *Supporting Growth. Supporting Growth* within our children is accomplished with four unique disciplines, *Exploring Possibilities, Assessing Desire, Securing Commitment,* and *Encouraging Progress.*

Pro-Active Parent Coaching Model

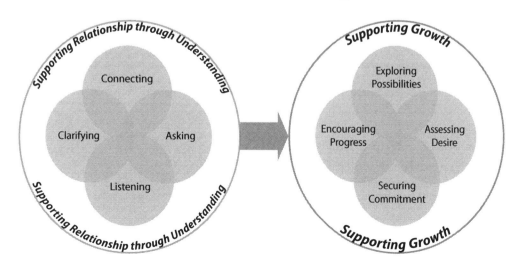

The *Pro-Active Parent Coaching* model emulates God's approach with us as His children. Establish relationship first, and then turn His attention toward supporting growth that is truly transformational.

> "My parents have used coaching for a few years and it has given me a great sense of vision for my life. We talk about my future, my gifts, talents, and the potential they see in me. They have also given me permission to reach for those goals and grow personally through trying and sometimes failing, but they are always there for me. My parents are excellent at affirming and believing in me."
>
> Jasmine, 17-year-old with coaching parents

God's First Priority

It's significant to note, God's first priority in our growth toward maturity is relationship. Reading through Scripture we notice this pattern emerge as God works with His people; He focuses on relationship, and when trust is established, He turns his attention to supporting our growth.

God initiates relationship with us by first offering Himself as the sacrifice necessary to restore relationship which was previously broken through the sin of disobedience. He then extends to us an invitation into relationship with Him through faith in His finished work. There is no pre-requisite, He does not ask us to clean up our act first, or change our lives before He will accept us. No, relationship is His first priority, He meets us where we are and invites us into relationship with Him. (Matthew 4:19; John 1:12; Ephesians 1:3-14; 2:1-10, Acts 9:1-18, 1 John 4:9-10)

Someone once said, "He loves us as we are but loves us too much to leave us that way." That's a pretty good description of our relationship with God, it is characterized by love and acceptance while providing a supportive and natural growth environment. Although God knows everything there is to know about us, particularly the areas in which we need to grow and mature, He does not demand immediate maturity or change within our lives. Instead, He patiently allows us to spiritually mature within our own natural growth patterns. For this we can be thankful, otherwise we would become overwhelmed, disheartened, and possibly just give up.

When relationship is established between God and ourselves, we witness an interesting pattern emerge.

- As relationship deepens, little by little, our trust for God increases.
- As our trust increases, we begin opening up, allowing Him to touch the deeper areas of our lives.
- As we open ourselves up to Him, we grow in our understanding that He is trustworthy.
- As we understand He is trustworthy, our relationship deepens and we open ourselves up to Him in an increasing manner.
- This promotes a healthy relational cycle, characterized by trust, openness and growth.

Relationship is the key to *Supporting Growth*, and if we are going to establish a healthy Parent Coaching Relationship with our children, it makes sense to emulate God's approach with us.

Commit to making relationship our priority and as we gain our children's trust they will most naturally invite us into the deeper areas of their lives and support their growth through coaching.

We must remember, access into the deeper areas of our children's lives comes by invitation only, and that invitation will most naturally come from a place of relationship in which they know they can trust us. Coaching gives us the tools we need to foster a healthy, interdependent, growth centered relationship - a relationship that can endure the trials and hardship that life naturally throws at us.

"Access into the deeper areas of our children's lives comes by invitation only."

Characteristics of God's Parent Coaching Relationship with Us as His Children

- Relationship is priority. He initiates, establishes and seeks relationship first and foremost.
- Continually offers unconditional love, accepting us as we are. There is no need to 'perform,' 'do,' or 'change' to receive His love.
- Continually focuses upon our growth potential.
- Releases responsibility according to our ability, and rewards with greater responsibility when faithful.
- Cooperates with our natural 'spiritual growth' patterns.
- Authentically listens to us.
- Gives us freedom to make decisions and carry responsibility/consequences of those decisions.
- Does not shelter us from all pain; but walks with us through pain to develop and strengthen character.
- Never abandons or turns His back upon us.
- When we falter and fail, His arms remain open, welcoming us back into relationship with Him.

Understanding and Applying the Pro-Active Parent Coaching Model

To help us understand and apply *Pro-Active Parent Coaching* within our parenting, let's revisit the parent coaching conversation from the previous chapter. I will break the process down into its individual components, so that you can see and understand what is taking place within my mind, the parent coach, as I support relationship and growth through the *Pro-Active Parent Coaching* model.

As you read this and the following coaching conversations within this book, keep in mind when Lynn and I began coaching our children it was not this natural or easy. With patience, practice, consistency and commitment, coaching has become a natural and normal part of our family life. Our children have appreciated and responded very well to our supporting them with this coaching model and I am confident it can do the same for you.

The first portion of this parent coaching conversation is purely relational. We do not have to be focussed upon a growth goal to appreciate the rich conversation we can have with our children. You will notice the elements of *Supporting Relationship through Understanding* at work from the outset of this conversation with one twist, it is Katelyn who has initiated the conversation and models the disciplines of *Connecting, Asking, Listening,* and *Clarifying* as she seeks a greater understanding of her Daddy. This highlights one of the benefits of coaching on a consistent basis within our families, we model healthy interpersonal relationship skills, and our children soon develop and begin using these disciplines themselves. This gives credibility to the old saying, "You can teach what you want, but you reproduce what you are!"

Coaching Conversation with Katelyn

Background
Although this conversation with Katelyn took a significant and surprising turn for us as parents, it's important to understand some of the background which fostered an environment that made this coaching conversation possible.

Some of our personal decisions include:

- Relating to our children in terms of their future, as responsible adults, as opposed to simply tolerating them until they move out.
- From the time our children could speak, we valued them by involving them in conversation on a regular basis. We practiced asking open questions, and listening as they answered, allowing them to fully share their thoughts with us.
- Involved them in decision making as opposed to unilaterally making decisions for them. This gave them an opportunity for input and crafting decisions, which strengthened relational bonds and respect between us.
- Model Transparency as a family value. If I truly desire my children to be open and honest with me, I must be open and honest with them. We have found that transparency has built a great sense of trust within our relationship together and has encouraged our children to open up and be honest with us in return.
- Relationship development is a priority. We have been intentional with our decisions and actions surrounding relational health. On a more practical side, we have set aside time, on a regular basis, specifically for the purpose of *Supporting Relationship*. Because of this, our moments of connection are more frequent and natural. Three specific examples you will see throughout the book are.
  - **Date Days:** These are times set aside specifically for one on one time with each of our children, which we began very early within their lives and continue today. Additionally, Lynn and I also have a 'date' each week, to keep our relationship healthy, and model for our children how they should treat and expect to be treated by their spouses.
  - **Family Outings:** We intentionally schedule regular recreational times together as a family.
  - **Dish Washing:** We take time washing the dishes by hand as opposed to using the dishwasher. This forces us to slow our pace and provides us with additional one on one time with the children on a regular basis.

The first discipline within our coaching model, *Supporting Relationship through Understanding,* is *Connecting.* Without connection, there will not be heartfelt conversation or openness within relationship. *Connecting* is the relational component that makes coaching possible. We have intentionally focussed upon the relational foundation, establishing trust within our relationship, that makes connection and conversations of this nature not only possible, but common.

All of these decisions flow from our desire as parents to *Support Relationship through Understanding* and can be summed up in what we call the *C.A.R.T.* principle of *Connecting: Consistency, Availability, Relevancy, and Transparency, which are outlined in greater detail in chapter 7.*

Notice this conversation has depth because of the trust that has been established in relationship and our willingness to be transparent with one another.

Conversation	What I am thinking.
"Dad, when you were younger, what did you want out of life?" Pleasantly surprised by this question, I turned, looked in her eyes and affirmed, *"That's a very good question, honey!"* then continued, *"You already have a good head start on me as a young person."* "In what way?" *"Well, for starters, I didn't have a Mom and Dad at home while I was growing up, I lived with your Nana but not your Grandpa. Unlike you, Katelyn, God wasn't a part of our lives and I didn't have a church family either. So at the time I didn't realize that life had any significant meaning or purpose to it. Never giving much thought about life beyond the present, I just kind of lived for myself in the moment. What felt right and good, what I wanted and desired; well, those are the kinds of things that I thought about and chased after."* "Like what Daddy?" *"Friends were a big deal to me, and having their acceptance and approval was very important. As I look back on my teen years though, I recognize that I wasn't a great friend to others. Still, I did have one thing going for me though - a very strong work ethic."* "What's a 'strong work ethic?" *"Well, that means I was a very hard worker."* "Ohh, OK." *"This helped me get and keep jobs as a young*	I thought, 'Wow, what a great question!' This has the potential to be an incredible conversation. This affirmation reassures that Katelyn is allowed to ask these questions and we will honor her by engaging in conversation with her about them. Katelyn is using the coaching model that we regularly employ in parenting. She has connected, is asking open questions and listening as I answer. Katelyn follows her curiosity by asking further questions so that she can understand what I am meaning and clarifies to ensure she does understand. I've made a conscious decision to model transparency and openly share with Katelyn because I want her to know that I am real and have made mistakes myself. There are obvious graphic details that I omit from the story, but I share enough that helps her understand what I

teen, which then gave me a taste for what money could do for me. Money gave me a great sense of security and freedom that I hadn't felt before. I bought a lot of my own stuff, and was quite proud of that. I bought my first car when I was 15, that way I'd have it when I turned 16 and got my license. I also bought my own street motorcycle when I was 16. I remember one big purchase that I made which my Mom really didn't approve of."

"What was that?"

"Another car, a Camaro Z28. Actually, before I bought it I asked her if she would mind. There was a part of me that wanted to honor her because I lived with her. But she did not want me to buy that car and let me know that she did not want it parked in her driveway. That is where our relationship was hurt, not because she said no, but because I went ahead and bought it anyway. We're fine now, as you know, but for a while, our relationship was pretty rough. Buying that car also meant I had to go in debt to purchase it, so I had to work very, very hard to keep up with the payments and that was tough as a teenager in school. But you know what, that wasn't the worst decision I made as a young teen."

"No?"

"Nope, the worst decision I made led me into an addiction to alcohol when I was just a couple of years older than you are now. In my mind I thought, 'It's my life, my body, my decision, it's no one else's business what I do!' I didn't give any thought at all to the fact that my decisions affect others around me."

Katelyn listened with interest as she slowly dried each dish and placed it carefully in its proper place within the kitchen cabinet. She paused for a moment, then turned and looked at me as a wry smile broke upon her face. Curiously I asked, *"What are you thinking right now?"*

She sheepishly looked at me, and responded with a giggle, "So, are you saying that you were selfish?"

Laughing, I reached for the next dish, affirmed her intuition and replied, *"Yes, young lady, if you boiled it all down, that is exactly what I am saying. It was all about me!"*

She laughed as she said, "Tell me more, Daddy."

"Well, honey, I am thankful that this is not the

have experienced. This brings a humanness and relatability into our relationship and hopefully when she needs to, she will come to me knowing I would understand.

I am sharing some very important things with Katelyn because I truly want her to consider life and the influence our decisions have upon ourselves and others. Knowing that I am sharing some things that might be a bit difficult for her to process, I allow moments when we are simply silent in conversation. This gives her an opportunity to fully consider what is being spoken without directing her thoughts elsewhere and losing its impact.

Instead of guessing what she may be thinking, I ask her to tell me what she is thinking.

I confirm her intuition and thoughts about my character at that time.

Following her invitation I continue to share. By keeping Katelyn in control

end of the story. You see, there was a significant event that took place when I was 18, which changed my thinking, and ultimately the direction of my life. One evening, while at a dance club, I had an interesting experience through which I knew God was trying to get my attention and have me think differently about Him and my life. In that moment, I recognized that many around me, including myself, were not really as happy as we pretended we were. That night I did a very important thing, I left the dance club and prayed, 'God, if you are real and you want me, reveal yourself to me!' And He did, He answered that prayer, but He didn't do it with a flash of light or something extraordinary. He did it in the most common way. He revealed Himself to me through other people, and you know what, I think He did that to show me that our lives do affect other people. Anyway, up to this point one young man had been asking me over and over to go to his youth ministry outings but I continually refused him. True to his character, the following week he asked me again. This time though, I accepted the invitation and went with him. I found myself there, with 30 other teenagers, having a great time, but with one major difference."

"What was that?"

"There was no alcohol."

"Cool."

"Yeah, it was cool. My curiosity about all of this was strong enough that I began attending this youth ministry and the church all the time. I actually developed a pretty good relationship with the youth pastor and many others in the church. For several months I hung with two crowds, the church family, and my dance club buddies. But, I began to realize that I was really living two lives and would have to make a decision, either serve God or turn my back on Him."

"At first, I chose the night clubs, but one evening, just after my 19th birthday I finally gave in to God. That was a huge thing for me and I learned a very valuable lesson about God that night."

"What was that?"

"Well, right then, I was kneeling at our toilet throwing up. I know it's not a real pretty picture, but I learned that God meets us wherever we are

of the conversation it allows her to go as deep as she wants to. She remains open and interested, asking me to tell her more.

I know this conversation has the potential to influence her thoughts and become a great teaching tool. I take the opportunity to share about my experience with God and how He began revealing Himself to me. This is a very personal story and Katelyn knows I am sharing something close to my heart. By doing so, I have made myself vulnerable, further strengthening our relationship together.

Knowing one day she will be wrestling with questions about God herself, I want to give her a personal example of how He meets us, wherever we are, when we call out to Him.

when we call out to Him."

"Wow."

"Yeah, that also showed me something else; He accepts us for who we are, and doesn't expect us to be all cleaned up first. You know, that night God took my addiction away and I haven't had a drop of alcohol from that moment to this. I knew without question that God accepted me and embraced me as one of His own. And I can honestly say that my whole outlook on life changed."

"In what way did it change?"

"Well, over time I began to understand that there was meaning to life and it was a whole lot more than simply buying stuff for me. I also recognized that our lives have an incredible influence upon others which will last way beyond this life, and I wanted that influence to be a positive one. God also helped me to understand and overcome my fear that all marriages would end in divorce. Because of this I risked asking your Mom to marry me and, of course, you know she said, 'Yes!' In time, God gave us three children who Mommy and Daddy love very, very much and He continues to lead us in helping other people by having us pastor a great church family here in Lively."

Katelyn listened intently as I shared. Taking it all in, she remained silent for a few moments then thoughtfully asked, "Daddy, what do you think I should do with my life?"

"That is a very important question to consider Katelyn," I affirmed. *"Before we jump into what you should do with your life, can I share another thought that might help you out a bit?"*

"Sure."

"In my understanding, God is more concerned with who we are becoming and our character, than He is with what we are doing. I think it is very important that we pay close attention to what He is doing within us; the character that He is forming through the things we experience; the gifts and talents that He has given to us; and the unique call that He places upon our lives. See, God is constantly forming and shaping us because what we do will flow naturally from who He is creating us to be. Katelyn, your life will naturally

This is a huge shift in conversation which shows me that she has taken to heart what has been spoken and is now considering her own life. Inside, I am screaming, 'YES!'

Three things are taking place here.
1. I affirm her desire and willingness to consider questions of this nature.
2. I quickly recall many teens and young adults I encountered throughout our ministry who struggled with 'God's will' for their life. Some believing that they had missed His perfect will and felt disillusioned and even hopeless because of it. I wanted to present Katelyn with a healthy approach to discerning God's will for

have an impact upon others, and if you're a young woman with great character, that impact will not only be long lasting, but positive too. As God continues to mold and shape you into the young lady He desires you to be, my guess is, He will present you with several options about what you can do with your life. Any of these options will be acceptable to Him and will fit well with who He has made you to be."

Pausing for a few moments here, I simply let silence fall, allowing her to consider, without distraction, the words that were spoken. After some time had passed, I continued by asking, *"Consider this, Katelyn; what have you noticed yourself thinking about a lot of the time?"*

After a few more moments of silence Katelyn opened up, "Well, I think a lot about the homeless, those who have no place to live, and no way to make money for food and stuff."

"Wow, that's interesting! Tell me more about this."

"Well, I would like to have a home with acreage, kind of like we have now, but a farm with a barn and horses, other animals and stuff like that. That way when I come across someone who doesn't have a home, they can come and live on the farm. They will be able to work with me, learn the skills and stuff they need to know so they can make it on their own. When they are ready and able they could move out and get their own home and stuff like that. That is something I've thought a lot about and I think I'd really like to do something like this. What do you think, Daddy?"

"What do I think? Well, Honey, this really excites me. It also tells me a lot about what God is forming in your character. Your compassion and desire to help others is something that I respect and admire. That makes me proud to be your Daddy. Can I ask you some more questions about this 'dream'?"

"Yeah, that's OK."

"As you think about having a farm and helping the homeless in this way, what kind of feelings does that stir up within you?"

"I feel good! I know I would love helping other people in that way too. You know there are lots of people who need help like this. I think it would be

her life, to help her avoid the common 'perfect will' trap, that many fall prey to. In light of this, I ask permission to delay her question and share another thought which may help her as she discerns what she should do with her life.

(An excellent book on this topic is "Christian Life Coaching" by Tony Stoltzfus)

3. We're beginning to transition from a great relational conversation to a coaching opportunity, through which, I can gain a greater understanding of what she is thinking, and support her growth.

The growth opportunity for Katelyn here is learning to discern God's voice within her life. If she can gain a grasp on this now, it will benefit her throughout her entire life.

Notice: I am surprised by this but invite her to tell me more about it so that I can gain an understanding of what she has been thinking about. By doing so, a whole new world opened up in this conversation, which may never have happened otherwise.

Here is where I had to exercise a lot of self control and stay focused upon Katelyn's dream development. I could easily get excited about this and begin strategizing and planning how to make this a reality, or worse yet, tell Katelyn what she needs to do and shortchange this growth opportunity for her. Knowing coaching will benefit her more than my telling her what to do; I opt to support her growth through coaching.

great, helping them get the skills they need while working on the farm. I also like horses, farms and stuff, so I would be able to help others, while doing something that I like. That'd be cool too."

"That's true! As you think about helping others in that way, is there anything else that comes to mind?"

"I just like the idea of being able to help people. It makes me feel good inside when I do, and they appreciate it too. That means a lot to me."

"What else can you tell me about this dream of yours?"

Katelyn gladly continued, sharing details about what the farm would look like, her plan for involving the homeless in chores and gardening and what they could learn so they could live out on their own. She listed all the animals she wanted on the farm but most importantly for me, she let me know, "You can be there to help out too, Dad; I will need a good maintenance man."

As Katelyn shared her thoughts, I intentionally slowed the pace of washing dishes in order to give her plenty of time to put into words what was within her heart. As we concluded, I thanked her for sharing and affirmed, *"You know, Katelyn, God may very well have placed this dream in your heart. What could you do to explore this a bit more and discover what He saying to you?"*

"Well, I could pray about it more."

"Definitely. Is there anything else that might help you understand what He is saying to you?"

"Umm, it may be a good idea to take some horse riding lessons too. That would help me know if I really like horses as much as I think I would."

"Those are both great possibilities. Is there anything else you can think of?"

- Reflective Pause -

"I could volunteer on a farm or at a Veterinary Clinic."

"Excellent, you're good at exploring possibilities. Is there one more thing you can think of?"

"No, I don't think so."

"OK, when you think of the possibilities you mentioned, praying, horse riding lessons, and volunteering, what would you like to do first?"

We want to foster an environment in which it is safe to dream. Asking her to share about her dream and listening as she does confirms this to Katelyn.

Having gained an *understanding* of Katelyn's thoughts about this dream, I want to encourage continued reflection upon it. This has the potential to become a great growth opportunity for her so I transition to the *Supporting Growth* coaching model. I affirm that God may have placed this dream within her heart and encourage her to discover what He might be saying. I begin by asking her to *Explore Possibilities* which will help her understand what God may be saying about this.

Continuing to *ask* in this way, communicates to Katelyn that she can indeed hear from and understand what God is saying to her. It further emphasizes the fact it is her dream, not Daddy's.

I am impressed with the possibilities she is coming up with. She has proven to be very creative.

I let her exhaust all of the possibilities she can think of, by asking, "Is there anything else?" Then move to *Assessing Desire* by asking, "What would you like to do first?"

Notice the shift from open questions to direct questions when asking for commitment.

"I could begin praying about it tonight"

"Yes, you could, is that something you are committed to doing?"

"Yes, I am, I'll do that just before I go to bed."

"That's a great start, honey. How do you feel about your decision?"

"I am excited about it. Thanks, Dad, for talking with me about this."

"You're very welcome. I look forward to hearing what God says to you about this dream. When would you like to talk about it again?"

"Our date day next week would work."

"Sounds great. Is there any other way Daddy can help you right now?"

"No, it's all good."

"OK, as you talk with God about this, just know I am here if you need me. Even if it is before our date day, you just have to let me know."

"OK Dad, thank you."

In order to make this a truly transformational growth experience for Katelyn, we must revisit this conversation. My desire is to provide a healthy accountability structure through which I can *Encourage her Progress* and help her navigate and apply learning to her life. So I commit to the process and ask for follow-up, 'When would you like to talk about it again?'

A time is secured to revisit the conversation and I affirm that I will be available to her if she needs me before this time.

The *Pro-Active Parent Coaching* model is a simple and practical tool, which makes coaching a natural approach to parenting. As you have just seen, coaching not only has the potential to increase relational bonds, but provides our children with an incredible support structure for their growth toward responsible adulthood.

What is the Difference between Coaching, Counseling, Teaching and Mentoring?

Coaching as a whole is a relatively new discipline and differs significantly from counseling, mentoring or teaching. Professional counselors are trained and certified to assist individuals who are experiencing emotional and/or mental health issues. Counselors will diagnose and assist their clients in resolving painful issues from the past to bring healing in the present. In contrast, coaches work from the present reality and help clients create an action plan to assist them in reaching their desired future. We must be clear on this point, coaching is NOT counseling. If your child has need of and would benefit from a professional counselor, we encourage you to seek help and assistance from one who is trained and certified to do so.

As a parent we will fulfill different roles to our children at different times within their development. We will teach, imparting knowledge or skill by giving instruction. At times we will mentor, allowing our child to draw upon our expertise and experience as they learn. Both of these, teaching and mentoring, draw upon our own resources as a parent, positioning us as the expert in the relationship.

Coaching, on the other hand, is future oriented and seeks to draw out of our children what God has already deposited within them. It encourages our children to make decisions, take responsibility for their own lives, and engage life experiences

"Coaching communicates that our children can indeed hear from and understand what God is saying to them."

for learning that is truly transformational. Additionally, coaching works in partnership with our children's *Natural Growth Patterns* assisting us in capturing and maintaining a hold upon their hearts; developing a healthy *inter-personal* relationship; and modeling a way of being that will impact all of their relationships throughout life. As our children mature, coaching will become the primary role we play within our parenting, creating a healthy *inter-dependent* relationship that can be enjoyed throughout adulthood.

> What if I didn't begin coaching my child while they were young, and they are already well into their teen years, is it too late to begin?
>
> Not at all! Many coaches I have spoken with didn't begin coaching their own children until they were in their teens simply because they did not know about or understand coaching and its benefits prior. There were two common benefits these parents shared about adding coaching to their parenting toolbox. a. Stronger relational bonds, and b. Their child's growth in responsibility.
>
> The absolute best time to begin adding coaching to your parenting is now, at whatever stage of development your child is in.

Moving Forward

Over the course of the next few chapters we will look at how *Pro-Active Parent Coaching* fits naturally within our parenting and will help us cooperate with our children's *Natural Growth Patterns* as they mature toward responsible adulthood.

In the second and third part of this book we will turn our attention to a more detailed look at both conversational models. Giving you an opportunity to see each element in action, and put it into practice within your own parenting. Enjoy your journey forward into *Pro-Active Parent Coaching*, you truly are the best coach your child could ask for.

Chapter

3

"Fathers, do not exasperate your children, so that they will not lose heart."
Colossians 3:21 (NASB)

Cooperating with our Children's Natural Growth Patterns Part 1

> "My parents don't trust me with anything, and for no reason. I mean, I haven't done anything to make them not trust me. But they treat me like I'm a little kid who isn't smart enough to do anything for myself. They say I am not old enough to make my own decisions, and they control everything about me, like friends, curfews, where I can and can't go. Pretty much everything! I honestly can't wait until I move out and can live my own life."
>
> "Pastor, we are at our wits end! It seems like our daughter is going off the deep end; she's resisting us at every turn. Accusing us of not trusting her, saying we are too controlling. We fear that she is going to rebel completely against us. Even though we keep telling her the decisions we make are for her own good, she just doesn't seem to grasp that we are not trying to hurt her, but keep her safe."
>
> A teen and her parents struggling in relationship

Here we see one family, living within the same household, having the same experiences, yet interpreting them entirely differently. This has become the unfortunate experience for many parents and begs the following questions;

What causes both children and parents to react like this?
What is really taking place that arouses such frustration?
What can I do to bring health back to this relationship?

Listening to both children and parents as they struggle through this critical time has brought a familiar and common issue to the surface. Statements like the ones above, and the conflict that often follows typically arises when our children's *Natural Growth Patterns* collide with a common but *Limiting Parenting Style*.

Chapter 3: Cooperating with our Children's Natural Growth Patterns Part 1   33

> # "What is *'it'* that our children are seeking independence from?"

This collision has left teens feeling resentful, and parents disillusioned. Children begin expressing a strong desire for *'independence'* and call parent's motives into question. Parents, on the other hand, are caught off guard with this sudden shift in their children's thinking and often misinterpret a child's actions as evidence of rebellion, and wonder,

> "What has happened to my once innocent child?"

With head spinning, and mind racing, parents try to regain control of the situation by tightening their grip. By doing so, parents may experience a greater push back from their child as the child begins to question, "Why are you so controlling?" The parent responds, "Don't you understand that it's because I love you and want what is best for you!?" This can lead to the misunderstanding and tension experienced between the parent and child quoted at the beginning of the chapter. Sometimes we as parents have inadvertently and subtly pushed our children away and are left wondering, "What in the world just happened?"

When we recognize this misunderstanding taking place, it is essential for us as parents to slow down, walk carefully, and seek understanding. This is essential if we are going to prevent unnecessary conflict, or build further resentment between us. Parent's hearts are often in the right place by loving, caring, providing, and protecting, but often go about this all wrong.

Understanding Our Child's Quest for Independence: Truth or Fiction?

Working with parents and teens during this critical stage of development, and seeing the pain that both parents and their children experience, aroused a serious question within my heart and mind.

> "What is *it* that our children are seeking independence from?"

In wrestling with this question I recognize that it is commonly believed and taught that adolescence is a period of time when our children are seeking independence. This is a time when they attempt to separate themselves from their parents and create their own individual identity. Listening as parents and educators alike talk about children in general growing toward independence, seeking independence, and pushing for independence, stirred some very conflicting thoughts within my mind.

If our children are truly seeking independence from us, how does this fit with God's intended design for people? Would this not be contrary to the way He fashioned us as people to function?

This set my mind to thinking about God's desire for people and relationships. We are created in God's image, and God Himself is the perfect example of an authentic interdependent relationship: Father, Son and Holy Spirit. This signifies that we have been designed and fashioned as interdependent beings not independent beings from the beginning.

Consider the creation account itself in Genesis 1 & 2. We read that, at the beginning of time as we know it, God in His amazing power, imagined and then spoke into existence all that we know in six successive days. At the conclusion of each day, He looked upon His handiwork and 'God saw that it was good.' The crown of creation, though, was man, created in His image and likeness. This is what separates us from the rest of creation.

Humankind was not spoken into existence like everything else, but rather, God took time apart from the rest of his work and got dirty. Kneeling in the soil, as a child might while building a sand castle at the beach, He fashioned the form of a man, but life had not yet entered him. I envision God kneeling beside the form that lies lifeless on the ground, and in His mind He imagines all that life will be for him, and smiles. Then leaning in toward the man, God places His mouth close to the mouth and nose on this form and breathes His spirit within it. There is a slight hush as the rest of creation watches in amazement, followed shortly by a gasp as the form breathes his first breath. God's life giving spirit entered and gave life to that form and he was called 'Adam'.

Man was then given stewardship of creation, to tend and provide care for what God entrusted to him. As God observed His handiwork, there was only one thing that stood out to Him as 'not good.' He observed Adam tending to and caring for the earth and said, 'It is not good for man to be alone, so I will make for him a suitable companion.' Just allow those words to sink in for a moment, 'It's not good for man to be alone,' *independent*, 'so I will make a suitable companion for him,' *interdependence*. God then caused a deep sleep to fall upon Adam and took a rib from his side, representing a side by side, mutually dependent relationship and fashioned for him a suitable companion and presented her to him. Adam embraced Eve as his partner and they enjoyed a healthy *interpersonal* relationship. It was not until after their sin of disobedience and the consequences of that sin, that this sin and separation would begin perverting and destroying God's original design for relationship. (See Genesis 1, 2 & 3)

We see within God's original design, the pattern of *interdependent* relationships, which were a direct reflection of His own character. Looking further we recognize that the word pictures He uses throughout Scripture to describe His children, 'the church,' 'the bride,' 'the family,' 'the body,' 'the building,' 'the nation,' also point to the unique characteristic of *interdependent* relationship.

> **"Our children's unique identity can be discovered within the context of interdependent relationships."**

This was the source of my own internal conflict. I found myself wrestling with what we are being taught about our children seeking *independence* and what I understood about God and His intended design for relationships.

So, what is the answer to the *'it'* question?
What is *'it'* that our children are
seeking independence from?
Is *'it'* really us, as parents?

I would like to encourage you with a loud and resounding NO, it is not us as parents they are seeking independence from. The opposite is in fact true; they desire and long for a healthy relationship with us as parents. I'd like to suggest that our children are seeking independence from another, but very significant, thing. They are seeking independence from the *Limiting Parenting Style* we employed when they were young children.

> **"Parents could mistake their child's natural push for freedom as rebellion, when in fact that may not be the case at all."**

The *Limiting Parenting Style* is one of 'doing for' and /or 'telling them what to do,' after they are capable of doing so themselves. Sometimes we simply do not allow our children to grow up, and holding on to our yesterdays, we continue to treat them as though they are children today, when in fact they are not. Other times, we may recognize and even hesitantly acknowledge that they are maturing, but fail to alter our parenting style as they do, and carry over this *Limiting Parenting Style* into adolescence, young adulthood and sometimes beyond. When we do this, it then becomes a genuine source of conflict between us and our children as they yearn for the freedom to express their growth and maturity.

The *Limiting Parenting Style* of 'doing for' and/or 'telling them what to do,' which although necessary when they are young children, sends a confusing and mixed message to them as they mature beyond childhood.

Understanding the Mixed Message

From birth our children are set upon a normal and *Natural Growth Pattern*. It is characterized by a healthy movement from complete dependence upon us toward responsible adulthood. As they mature, their *Natural Growth Patterns* begin sending internal messages like;

> You are growing and maturing.
> Your abilities are increasing.
> You can begin handling some of your own problems,
> make decisions and take responsibility.
> Begin exercising this!

On the other hand, our *Limiting Parenting Style* is communicating something entirely different;

> You're still a child.
> You're not capable of doing this on your own.
> You're not ready to handle problems, make decisions,
> or carry responsibility on your own.
> You still need me to tell you what to do!

Herein we experience the collision between our children's *Natural Growth Patterns* and our *Limiting Parenting Style,* naturally creating tension between us. During this time, parents could mistake their child's natural push for freedom as rebellion, when in fact that may not be the case at all, causing unnecessary relational conflict between the parent and child.

To help you visualize this, observe the diagrams on the following page.

Natural Growth Patterns
Natural Growth Pattern from Birth to Responsible Adulthood

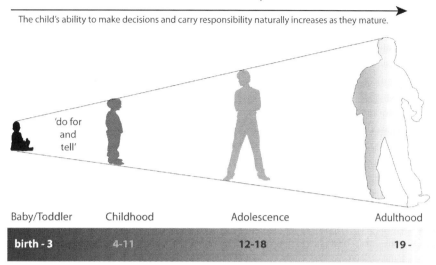

Birth sets the child on a Natural Growth Pattern that promotes progressive movement from complete dependence upon the parent toward an ability to manage their own life as a responsible adult. As the child matures, their desire and ability to make decisions and take responsibility naturally increases.

Limiting Parenting Style
'do for and tell'

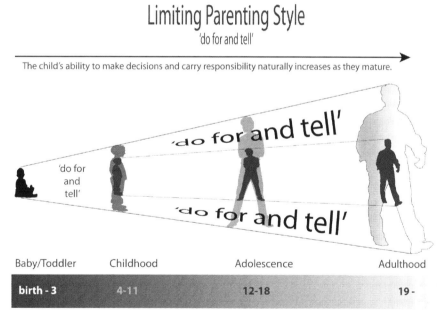

The child's growing ability and their internal need is for much less direction than the parent is giving here. This creates an internal tension within the child which will become more pronounced as they mature: Their desire for the freedom to exercise their own growing abilities, collides with the Limiting Parenting Style to 'do for and tell' them what to do. If this continues the child will either, a. Yield control to the parent completely and develop an unhealthy dependent relationship which can continue well into adulthood, or b. Seek freedom to exercise their growing abilities by severing relationship with the parent and developing an unhealthy independent relationship.

The *Limiting Parenting Style* to *'do for and tell'* our children what to do, is one we naturally become accustomed to upon welcoming a new baby into our home. Their complete dependence upon us is quickly recognized. We feed them, clothe them, protect them, pick up after them, nurture them and, ahem, change their dirty bottoms. It becomes natural and second nature to 'do for and tell' when our children are young, as a result we can inadvertently continue doing so much longer than we should.

The *Natural Growth Pattern* of our children is one of gradual movement from complete dependence upon us toward responsible adulthood. As our children mature, their ability to make decisions and carry responsibility does, as well. This makes it necessary that we step into a different parenting role, giving them the freedom they need to mature in a healthy manner, while resisting the urge to continue 'doing for and telling them' what to do.

Children will only mature toward responsible adulthood when we give them the freedom to make decisions, take responsibility, initiate action, solve problems, face challenges, and experience some pain along the way. Otherwise, we create an unhealthy dependence upon us as parents, or, push them away, causing them to seek freedom to exercise their growing abilities elsewhere.

Reflection

Take a moment and look at the diagram on the previous page. Compare a child's *Natural Growth Pattern* with the *Limiting Parenting Style*.

Place a child of approximately 14 years of age on the developmental scale and consider what is taking place within them if the parent continues to 'do for and tell' as if they were a young child.

- What is their likely reaction . . .
  a. Relationally with the parent?
  b. Developmentally as they mature?

- What internal tension(s) might the child be experiencing at this time?
- In what way(s) might this serve to foster 'independent' thinking by the child?

Think about our purpose in parenting, "To prepare responsible adults for life beyond the shelter of our home."

- How effective will this parenting style be in fulfilling that purpose?
- Place your child's age in the appropriate place upon the scale, then ask yourself the same questions from above.

Is There Hope?

Can a middle ground be met?
Can this collision be avoided?
Can the damage be minimized?
Can the damage be repaired,
if this collision has already taken place?

The good news is YES, it is possible! But it will require

Self Control,
Understanding,
Intentionality,
Time, and
Effort!

> The way they parent me has helped me to see them more like fellow people, instead of rulers with vast amounts of laws. They involve me in making decisions about my boundaries, consequences, and future. This helps me to relate my heart to them more easily, and treat them both like friends instead of enemies. As I have grown, they have steadily included me more and more in the decision making process, and have also given me more freedom in making my own decisions. Because of that, I feel more prepared for life but also have a good relationship with them.
>
> Shayla, 16 with coaching parents

The best way to maintain focus and intentionality as parents is to understand our purpose in parenting. Are we supposed to shelter our children from all pain, or, are we preparing responsible adults for life beyond the shelter of our homes?

Our answer to that question will greatly impact how we navigate the journey between our child's birth and their launching out from our homes. Cooperating with our children's *Natural Growth Patterns* will require a change of parenting styles as our children mature. Moving from a *Limiting Parenting Style* to an *Empowering Parent coaching Style* will foster a healthy interpersonal relationship that we can enjoy with our children throughout life. Further, it creates a supportive growth environment in which our children can rise up and reach their God-given potential. As our children mature we do not abandon our parental responsibilities: instead we alter our parenting style in a way that works in cooperation with our children instead of against them.

"Children will naturally mature toward responsible adulthood when we give them the freedom to do so."

An Empowering Approach

Observe the following parenting model which works in partnership with our children's *Natural Growth Patterns* creating a healthy interpersonal relationship that can be carried throughout adulthood.

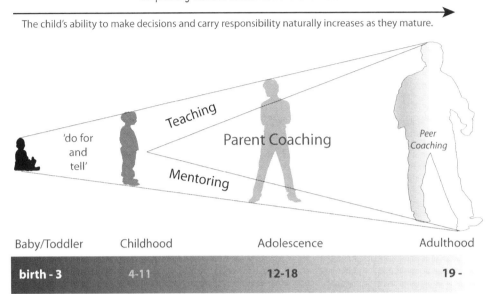

Empowering Parenting Style
Cooperating with the Child's Natural Growth Patterns

The child's ability to make decisions and carry responsibility naturally increases as they mature.

'do for and tell'

Teaching

Parent Coaching

Mentoring

Peer Coaching

Baby/Toddler	Childhood	Adolescence	Adulthood
birth - 3	4-11	12-18	19 -

The child's growth and maturity is welcomed by the parents' willingness to give increasing freedom and responsibility that keeps pace with the child's natural ability. Changing parenting roles as the child needs, helps the parent work in cooperation with their natural growth patterns and encourages the child's growth toward responsible adulthood. By doing so the parent creates a supportive environment for healthy relationship and growth for their child, making the transition between developmental stages more natural for both parent and child alike. As the parent transitions from 'doing and telling,' to teaching, mentoring, and parent coaching this interdependent relationship can be carried through adulthood as peer coach when the child leaves the shelter of the home.

The *Empowering Parenting Style* acknowledges that there is a season in our children's lives in which we legitimately 'do for and tell' our children what and how to do, but, this is a relatively short season within their lives! To prepare our children as responsible adults, we will need to be flexible and employ different 'parenting roles' throughout their growth and development and resist the temptation to continue 'doing for and telling them what to do.'

> "I believe I will have a long lasting, great relationship with my parents for many reasons, one of which being because they know how to treat me with respect. They respect me, believe in me, and hear me out. Not to say they aren't firm or let me control them but we have a relationship of mutual respect for one another."
> Jasmine, 17

Our role in parenting will naturally change depending upon our children's need at the moment. In some cases we will teach, imparting knowledge, at other times we will mentor, allowing them to glean from our experience, and often we will coach. It is important to note that as our children grow in maturity, they will need us to step back, releasing more responsibility and give greater freedom to them. The heart, skills and disciplines of *Pro-Active Parent Coaching* will help us, as parents, do this with greater ease. In turn, we will help our children leverage their experiences for learning that is truly transformational. In doing so, we create a healthy *interpersonal* relationship that honors our children's unique God-given identity.

Independence: An internal drive to be free from the influence, guidance, and/or parental control, while developing one's own set of values and unique identity. This enables them to declare themselves *independent,* being sovereign over and having control of their own life.

Interdependence: Each member is mutually dependent upon one another for healthy growth and development, while maintaining one's own individual identity. Interdependence creates a healthy sense of belonging, and honors the value each individual brings to the relationship. One's unique identity can be discovered and celebrated within the context of interdependent relationship.

Reflection

Take a moment and look at the diagram on the following page. Compare a child's *Natural Growth Pattern* with the *Empowering Parenting Style* which embraces the child's growth patterns and gives them freedom to exercise their growing abilities.

Place a child of approximately 14 years of age on the developmental scale and consider what is taking place within them as their parent gives freedom and responsibility in accordance to their growing ability to manage it.

- What benefit might this have for the child?
- What is their likely reaction . . .
  a. Relationally with the parent?
  b. Developmentally as they mature?
- In what way might this serve to foster a healthy 'interdependent' relationship with our child?

Think about our purpose in parenting, "To prepare responsible adults for life beyond the shelter of our home."
- How effective will this parenting style be in fulfilling that purpose?

Place your child's age on the scale in the diagram above and consider the following.

- In what ways can I begin giving freedom and responsibility now?
- How will this begin preparing them for life beyond my household?
- What will I commit to doing?

Comparing the Child's Natural Growth Pattern and the Empowering Parenting Style

Natural Growth Patterns
Natural Growth Pattern from Birth to Responsible Adulthood

The child's ability to make decisions and carry responsibility naturally increases as they mature.

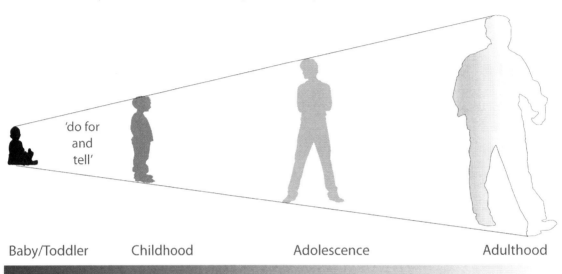

'do for and tell'

Baby/Toddler	Childhood	Adolescence	Adulthood
birth - 3	4-11	12-18	19 -

Empowering Parenting Style
Cooperating with the Child's Natural Growth Patterns

The child's ability to make decisions and carry responsibility naturally increases as they mature.

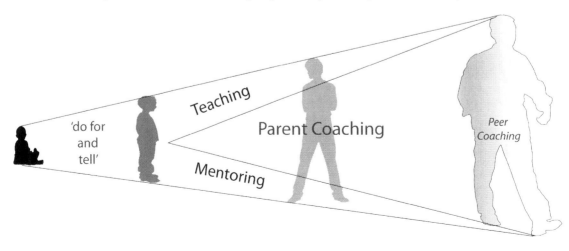

'do for and tell'

Teaching

Parent Coaching

Mentoring

Peer Coaching

Understanding and working in cooperation with our children's *Natural Growth Patterns* will foster a supportive relational and growth environment, giving an overall sense of cooperation between us and our children. In effect, embracing *Pro-Active Parent Coaching* will help us cultivate a healthy relationship with our children, and reduce the unnecessary conflict that comes through misunderstanding our children's *Natural Growth Patterns* and their growing desire to carry responsibility.

Exercise

Set aside time this week to speak with your child. Let them know that you truly want to understand them in a greater way so that you can give them the freedom they need to mature as responsible young adults.

You could begin by saying something like . . ."I've been thinking about what might be going on inside of you and realize that I may have misunderstood some of your comments and actions. My first thought was that you were becoming rebellious but I realize now that I could be wrong in my judgment and there may be something else going on. Could you help me understand where you are at in your need for greater freedom, responsibility and input in decision making?"

- "Tell me about your personal need for freedom, responsibility and decision making."
- "In what ways have I supported your growth in maturity at this point?"
- "What can I do or say differently that will support you and show respect for your growth in maturity?"
- "What guidelines should we set up to keep you safe but not shelter you too much?"
- "What are you looking forward to as we work together on this?"

"Two of the greatest gifts we can give our children are - responsibility and the freedom to grow in it."

Cooperating with our Children's Natural Growth Patterns Part 2

Loosening our grip on control, releasing responsibility, allowing our children to make decisions, and experience the pain of failure, may be among the hardest things for parents to do. However, these are the very ingredients essential for our child's healthy development toward responsible adulthood.

Reflection

When you consider the above statement . . .
- What thoughts immediately come to mind?
- What feeling does that stir up within you?
- At what point do you most agree with this statement?
- Where do you experience the most internal resistance to this statement?

As loving parents we have a natural tendency to offer solutions, solve our children's problems, and protect them from painful experiences because we genuinely desire to help. In our quest to offer the love and support we feel they need, we can subtly and unintentionally push them away from us.

Great Parent Coaches have a deep love for their children and an overall desire for their wellbeing which transcends the present and focuses upon their future. Parent Coaches understand that transformational learning takes place through pivotal life experiences coupled with significant relationships that encourage our children to reflect and apply learning to life. Simply telling our children what *we think* they need to know,

> "You cannot teach a child to take care of himself unless you will let him take care of himself. He will make mistakes, and out of these mistakes will come his wisdom."
> Henry Ward Beecher

and continuing to '*do for*' them, does not facilitate the growth they require for life beyond the care and shelter our homes provide.

Transitioning our parenting style will be easier for some than others, but with commitment it can be experienced by anyone.

Consider the words of Sharon who shares about her transition to coaching from telling.

> "It took concentration, intentionality and hard work to remember to ask questions that were open and not closed. Solution oriented questions were also hard to stay away from because as a parent I had a tendency to want them to do things a certain way. Actually it was pretty exhausting for awhile until asking open questions became more second nature."
>
> "I had to learn to be patient while waiting for their answers as they reflected and learned how to put in words what they were thinking and feeling. It made me work on the transition from child to young adult in my own mind, and realize that God was working in their lives. But it's been worth it, because we are so much closer emotionally; we share so much deeper; and we can do both much more quickly."
>
> Sharon Wildman, Coach and mother of two adult children
> Stubborn Pursuits Ministries

Transitioning can be tough and there will be a temptation to revert back to a 'telling model' of parenting by offering solutions to our children because:

- We may do it as a manner of habit.
- It may simply be because it is familiar and therefore more comfortable for us.
- It may be a time issue, "It's always much quicker if I simply do it myself or tell them what and how to do things."
- It's much easier to just tell them.
- Or, for some, it may be a matter of needing to maintain control.

Whatever form our temptation takes, it is our responsibility to resist the temptation to revert back, and commit to a new parenting style that will benefit both ourselves, and our children over the long haul.

A Note on Control and Freedom

Control is an interesting thing: the more we give away, the more we receive in return. It is a universal truth in life. Parents who tend to maintain a tight hold on control and fail to release it gradually to their children, typically end up losing what control they already had. Refusing to give greater freedom and release control to our children, in accordance with their growing ability, creates a natural tension within their lives as they mature. This builds within them a stronger desire to resist or push back in order to gain a sense of freedom and control of their life.

When Should I Jump in and Help?

It is NOT our responsibility to shelter our children from all pain. Pain provides some incredible learning experiences through which our children's character is forged. We do however have a responsibility to protect them from harm that does not serve their growth and learning.

We jump in and help when they could lose their life, be drastically injured, or know that they are in a situation that they cannot handle on their own. Always bear in mind, everything we take care of for our children, they will not develop the ability to care for on their own. As we consider jumping in and helping, as much as possible, maintain a coaching posture by first asking for permission to get involved and receiving their invitation to do so. This will honor them as an individual and allow them to maintain a sense of dignity and control within their life.

Squash or Oak Tree?

In our age of quick fixes and solutions, we often forget that it takes time and effort to grow responsible adults. There is a story about James Garfield that illustrates this point well. The story points out that prior to becoming President of the United States, Garfield was the principal of Hiram College in Ohio. When a father asked if the course of study couldn't be simplified so his son could finish school sooner, Garfield replied, "Certainly. But it all depends on what you want to make of your boy. When God wants to make an oak tree, He takes a hundred years. When he wants to make a squash, He requires only two months."[1]

"Quick and easy does not build the quality of character, or relationship needed, to sustain them throughout life."

What do we want to make of our children? Quick and easy does not build the quality of character, or relationship needed, to sustain them throughout life. Committing to the long haul, understanding that we are helping our children build character that will sustain them throughout life, will be much better for our children than a quick or easy fix could ever be.

As parent coaches we are intentional about *Supporting Relationship and Growth*, and work in cooperation with our children's *Natural Growth Patterns*, helping them to:

> Think deeper,
> > Reflect more,
> > > Dream of possibilities,
> > > > Take action, and
> > > > > Grow through experience.

We pray that God brings the people and circumstances into their lives that will build the character they need, actively watch for teachable moments and position ourselves as their coach when they need someone to talk to.

The Age Trap

The question remains then, when do I begin coaching my child? One of our greatest stumbling blocks is our own tendency to think in terms of specific ages as opposed to ability.

"What is the right age at which to begin?"
"Is my child old enough?"
"My child is not ready!"
"They are too young to make decisions on their own."
"When they are older I will give them more freedom and responsibility."

Age and maturity are not necessarily synonymous, but the opposite is also true; youth and immaturity are not necessarily synonymous, either.

> Consider, for a moment, the top complaints today's teens have about their parents.
> - Parents try to make decisions for them.
> - Parents are too controlling.
> - Parents are over-protective.
> - Parents try to live vicariously through them.
> - Parents love sometimes feels conditional.
> - Parents have unrealistic expectations, or they expect perfection.
> - Parents project their own fears and insecurities upon them.
> - Parents don't practice what they preach.[2]

If we get caught in the age trap, we have greater potential to miss recognizing, acknowledging, and affirming the abilities our children currently have, in whatever stage of development they are in. Blinded by this we may continue to 'do for and tell' them what to do, creating an internal tension within them, and prompting an honest questioning of our motives.

"Why can't I make some of these decisions on my own?"
"Why doesn't my opinion matter?"
"May I please decide? I am willing to live with the consequences."

Innocent questions and statements like these, are simply indicators letting us know that their development toward responsible adulthood is well underway, and a change in our parenting style is needed. We can no longer simply tell them what to do. We must begin involving them in decisions and handling responsibility, or risk pushing them away.

Often, the questions for us are:

How and when do I begin?
If age isn't the primary consideration, what is?
When I recognize that it's time to begin, how do I go about it?

We'll consider these questions by observing a coaching session with Robert, a Dad with 2 children, as he wrestles with this very topic. Afterward, we will turn our attention to a Biblical Model of releasing responsibility.

In Office Coaching Session with Robert

"Greg, I'm struggling with something. My son Stephen is constantly telling me that I am controlling and don't trust him enough. I sense tension growing between us and I, ah, really don't want to go down that road. It's got me thinking about how old he is and at what age I should consider relaxing my control a bit and give him more freedom with decisions and such.

"Well Robert, the good news in all of this is you're a normal Dad! How can I best serve you through this time?"

"You know I value your friendship and opinion, so I was wondering what you think about this whole thing. What would be a good age to start giving him more freedom?

"Well, what would you think if I said, "It's really not a question of age at all"?

"Honestly, I'm not sure what I think of that because it seems like a matter of age to me. I was seventeen when I moved out on my own and began making decisions for myself. Stephen is only eleven and there are quite a few years at home yet before he heads out on his own and becomes an adult."

"Do you mind if we talk about your experience a bit?"

"Yeah, sure, that's no problem."

"You mentioned you were 17 when you headed out on your own; tell me about your experience with that."

"Honestly?"

"Of course."

"Well, at first I was pretty excited about being out from under my parent's control. I felt like I had finally found the freedom I had been looking for. I could make my own decisions, live my own life and finally do what I wanted to do without always dreading that long-drawn-out lecture from my parents. Actually, I was really popular with my friends, too, which was great! Well, at least for a while, then reality hit me hard."

"What do you mean by 'reality hit me hard?'"

"Well, I really had no clue how much money it took to survive out of my parents' home on my own. As a teen, I never considered the cost of living. The rent, electricity bills, insurances, food, vehicles, etc, etc, etc. When I was at home, my parents took care of all of that. They were very generous with us kids, so I never really considered the cost of even the simple things. I guess I really took all of that for granted when I was living at home. Financially, I was a wreck. I couldn't keep ahead of my bills and ended up having to take several odd jobs to maintain my lifestyle. As a result, I crashed and burned, I just couldn't juggle it all. It wasn't until creditors started calling that I admitted I had a problem. To tell the truth, I never did tell my parents how bad it got, because I was just too embarrassed by the whole thing."

-Lengthy pause -

"You know, looking back, I made a lot of decisions that I am ashamed of today."

"That's hard. You've had some tremendous experiences in your life. Do you mind

if I ask another question?"

"Yeah sure, go ahead."

"Thinking about those experiences today, what positive effect did they have upon you?"

"That's an interesting twist. Well, there is no doubt in my mind that these experiences marked me for life. As difficult as they were to go through, one positive thing is that they forced me to get help and learn to manage my money. Another positive thing is that I learned to take some time and weigh my decisions, as opposed to being so impulsive. You know what, some of the greatest lessons I've learned came through my most trying years."

"That's great insight. Some of the greatest lessons you have learned have come through your most trying years. We can go a couple of directions here. We could continue talking about the lessons you've learned after leaving home and their impact upon you, or, keeping all of this in mind we could return to your original question regarding Stephen. What would you like to do?"

"My concern right now is Stephen, so let's go back to him."

"OK, he is 11 years old now, correct?"

"Yes."

"With the insight and lessons you have learned through your own experience, what would it look like for Stephen to leave home in just 6 or 7 years, prepared for what life might throw at him?"

- Thoughtful silence –

"That's an interesting question. Truth be known, the first 11 years are a blur for me, and it is probably safe to say the next 6 or 7 will fly by, too."

- Thoughtful silence.-

"Well, for starters, he would have a grasp on money, knowing its value and how to manage it. Stephen would also have an understanding of the consequences of his decisions. He'd have an ability to sit down and thoughtfully consider the pros and cons of a decision prior to making it, hopefully making wiser decisions in the long run. Also he'd have the ability to manage his time well, balancing work and play. I felt I missed out in that way. I believe if he only had a grasp on these three things it would give him greater confidence as he moves out of our home and starts life on his own."

"Those are great. Does anything else come to mind?"

"Yeah, one more thing stands out to me."

"What's that?"

"I would like him to know that no matter what he gets himself into, he could come to me knowing that I would not condemn him, but I am standing in his corner rooting for him."

"That's great! How do you feel about your description of Stephen as he leaves from home and launches out on his own?"

"I'm stoked! I'm thinking this kid has a great chance of being successful and navigating life, an even better chance than I did myself."

"Now imagine yourself years down the road: Stephen has developed strength in

these areas. He's not perfect, but he has a growing ability with these things you described. You're standing at his college or university dropping him off for his first week of classes. What are you thinking, as a Dad?"

"I am thinking, 'Man, he's going to be OK' I know that he has grown in his abilities and although he may make mistakes, he has the confidence to grow through them and not let them beat him down. I'm actually excited about the prospect of his future."

"That's great. Now let's journey back for a moment and focus on your original question - when do you think is the best time to begin giving more freedom to Stephen?"

Smiling now, Robert begins. "When I first came in here, I had hoped you'd tell me what you thought and I was even hoping that would be later on, when he is a teen and has developed more. But as we've talked about this, I am beginning to see this more as a process than an event. I shouldn't wait any longer but begin now! If I relax my grip a bit and give him more freedom, allow him to make some decisions, it will give him the experience he needs before leaving our home on his own. I'd also get to show him that I respect him and support him by being there when he messes up, not to beat him up, but support him through it. That would mean the world to me."

"That's excellent! So what is your first action step?"

"Well, I'm going to go home and have a heart to heart talk with Laura and share with her what I discovered today. Then I'd like to sit down together as a family, Laura, Stephen, Samuel and I, and determine what appropriate responsibilities we can begin giving each of them. I don't want to waste any more time."

"Fantastic! Is there anything else you need from me as you move forward with this?"

"No, I'm good. I think this will be great and appreciate you challenging my thinking today."

"You're very welcome! One more thing - would you do me a favour?"

"Sure what is it?"

"As this unfolds for you, would you let me know how things are progressing for your family? I'd be encouraged to hear it."

"Absolutely, that's not a problem at all."

"Thank you, I look forward to talking again and hearing about your progress."

Robert's decision to begin cooperating with Stephen's natural growth and development will give Stephen valuable experience from which to draw upon as an adult. Even at 11 years of age Stephen can begin developing his ability to explore possibilities, tap into his desire, and take committed action as his parents support his growth. In this way he will be better prepared for life when he launches out from Robert and Laura's home. The benefit of this coaching approach is that it makes it possible to continue a healthy interpersonal relationship after Stephen leaves home, as Robert and Laura transition from Parent Coach to Peer Coach.

If we begin coaching our children *prior to* adolescence it will make the transition from childhood, to adolescence, and into adulthood much smoother for both us and our children. This will position us as partners within their growth and development, encouraging a healthy interdependence, as opposed to pushing them away.

Coaching will better prepare our children to handle more complex problems and decisions that will face them as they mature, preparing them for life beyond our households. And when it comes to that day, when they launch out from our homes, it will also be easier on us, too, because we will have seen that our children are well prepared for the world they are entering into.

A Biblical Model for Releasing Responsibility

"Releasing responsibility in a healthy manner involves fostering an environment in which it is safe for our children to experiment with and grow in decision making."

The Biblical model for releasing responsibility is focused upon an individual's ability and faithfulness to administer what is entrusted to their care, as opposed to specific age requirements. Throughout Scripture we see that children and youth are valued members of the body. They are validated, called, gifted, equipped and expected as adults are, to steward well what God has deposited within them (1 Corinthians 12). Timothy, a young man, was admonished not to let others despise him because of his age, but rather to set an example by living a godly life and faithfully administering the gifts he had received(1 Timothy 4:12). The boy Samuel was encouraged that he could discern what God was saying to him and was called by God from a very tender age (1 Samuel 3). David, having developed in character as a young shepherd boy, killed Goliath as a teen (1 Samuel 17), and Mary was almost certainly a teenager when the angel announced that she was chosen as the person who would give birth to Jesus (Luke 1 & 2). Throughout Scripture we see that age is not the focus for releasing responsibility; rather responsibility is given according to ability, regardless of age.

This is clearly depicted in the parable of the three servants'. Please take note of the added emphasis (emphasis mine) as you read through this passage of Scripture.

Again, the Kingdom of Heaven can be illustrated by the story of a man going on a long trip. He called together his servants and entrusted his money to them while he was gone. 15 He gave five bags of silver to one, two bags of silver to another, and one bag of silver to the last—***dividing it in proportion to their abilities.*** He then left on his trip. 16 "The servant who received the five bags of silver began to invest the money and earned five more. 17 The servant with two bags of silver also went to work and earned two more. 18 But the servant who received the one bag of silver dug a hole in the ground and hid the master's money. 19 "After a long time their master returned from his trip and called them to give an account of how they had used his money. 20 The servant to whom he had entrusted the five bags of silver came forward with five more and said, 'Master, you gave me five bags of silver to invest, and I have earned five more.' 21 "The master was full of praise. 'Well done, my good and faithful servant. ***You have been faithful in handling this small amount, so now I will give you many more responsibilities. Let's celebrate together!'*** 22 "The servant who had received the two bags of silver came forward and said, 'Master, you gave me two bags of silver to invest, and I have earned two more.' 23 "The master said, ***'Well done, my good and faithful servant. You have been faithful in handling***

this small amount, so now I will give you many more responsibilities. Let's celebrate together!' 24 "Then the servant with the one bag of silver came and said, 'Master, I knew you were a harsh man, harvesting crops you didn't plant and gathering crops you didn't cultivate. 25 I was afraid I would lose your money, so I hid it in the earth. Look, here is your money back.' 26 "But the master replied, 'You wicked and lazy servant! If you knew I harvested crops I didn't plant and gathered crops I didn't cultivate, 27 why didn't you deposit my money in the bank? At least I could have gotten some interest on it.' 28 "Then he ordered, 'Take the money from this servant, and give it to the one with the ten bags of silver. 29 ***To those who use well what they are given, even more will be given, and they will have an abundance.*** But from those who do nothing, even what little they have will be taken away. 30 Now throw this useless servant into outer darkness, where there will be weeping and gnashing of teeth.' Matthew 25:14-30 (NLT)

In relation to releasing responsibility, parents can learn a lot from the Biblical Model seen within this passage of Scripture.

Principles for Releasing Responsibility

1. ***Foster an environment that minimizes fear.*** 'Fear of the master' was cited as the reason the third servant did nothing with what was entrusted to his care. For our children, fear of how we will respond to them can be paralyzing and keep them from stepping out and taking responsibility. We have the potential to remove that fear through the gift of relationship by:

    *   Showing unconditional love at all times.
    *   Acknowledging our love is for them, not their performance.
    *   Creating a culture of responsibility for everyone in the family.
    *   Expecting faithfulness, not perfection.
    *   Fostering an environment in which it is safe to risk and make mistakes.
    *   Emphasizing that failure is a learning opportunity. Simply because our children may fail at something, it does ***not*** make them a failure.
    *   Showing unconditional love at all times.

    Taking these steps creates an environment that encourages our children toward growth and maturity and minimizes the potential fear of how we will respond to them. You'll notice that these steps begin and end with 'showing unconditional love.' 1 John 4:18 states, "Where God's love is, there is no fear, because God's perfect love drives out fear. It is punishment that makes a person fear, so love is not made perfect in the person who fears." (NCV) When our children know that our love for them is unconditional, it frees them from unnecessary and limiting fears.

2. ***Release responsibility according to ability.*** Every child has ability in some area. The bigger question is, 'What are my child's abilities right now?' When this is determined, we release responsibility to them that complements what they can currently manage. The health of this approach is seen in the following:

    *   It is *responsible;* it allows our children to mature and grow in their abilities as opposed to simply cutting them loose at a predetermined age.

- It is *realistic*; we only ask our children to be responsible for what they can honestly manage.
- It is *revealing*; we learn through this process what our children are truly capable of.
- It is *rewarding*; it builds self confidence within our children as they prove faithful.
- It is *relational*; it takes place within our own loving care and observation.

Of course this requires an intimate knowledge and honest acknowledgment of our child's unique abilities, but the time we spend together discovering this will prove to be a wonderful time of relational connection.

3. ***Evaluate based upon faithfulness.*** Faithfulness is our evaluation tool, not performance, or unrealistic expectations. In this parable the expectation was simply that the servants would administer their talents faithfully. He did not expect the one with two bags of silver to function at the same level of performance as the one with five, but each one was simply evaluated based upon their own ability. The key is to focus upon each child's unique ability making the evaluation fair and realistic, as opposed to comparing them to ourselves, or others, creating unhealthy and unrealistic expectations.

4. ***Acknowledge and celebrate faithfulness.*** As our children mature and grow in these areas it is appropriate to celebrate their growth in maturity. Discovering a unique and meaningful way to acknowledge our child's growth is an incredible encouragement to them which continues to build their confidence and desire to grow in responsibility.

5. ***Reward by giving more responsibility.*** There is no greater affirmation that our children can receive than gaining our trust and having us release more responsibility to them. As our children mature and grow in their ability, we must honor that and celebrate their faithfulness and growth by giving more freedom.

Releasing responsibility in a healthy manner involves fostering an environment in which it is safe for our children to experiment with and grow in decision making, carrying responsibility and experiencing the consequences of those decisions. This is best done within the loving care of their Parent Coach who facilitates deeper reflection, helping them make connections between what they are experiencing and how they can apply learning to their lives.

Examples
- Your child has shown responsibility and faithfulness with arriving home at curfew for an extended period of time. To honor them and celebrate their faithfulness you could initiate a conversation with them highlighting their growth in responsibility. In the course of conversation you provide encouragement and affirmation verbally and could extend their curfew as a reward for their faithfulness.
- Your child has shown responsible behavior and is now old enough to be left unattended for short periods of time. You could honor them and celebrate their responsibility by highlighting their growing ability and beginning to leave them 'unattended' for short periods of time.

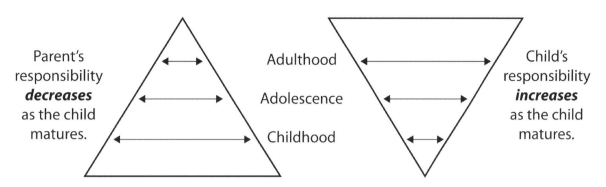

As our children mature toward adulthood, their desire for and ability to carry responsibility naturally increases. Two of the greatest gifts we can give our children are - responsibility and the freedom to grow in it.

Questions to Consider as You Begin

- In light of this chapter how would I describe the home environment that my child and I are currently experiencing?
- What life skills will my child need when they leave home?
- How can I begin encouraging the development of these skills now?
- What is my child honestly capable of handling today that I could begin giving responsibility for?
- How much responsibility am I willing to risk giving them as I discern what their abilities are?
- Are my own fears holding them back?
- In what ways can I begin involving my child in decision making processes, to allow them to have greater input in and taking ownership of their decisions?
- In what ways have they already carried responsibility and proven themselves capable and faithful to do so? How can I affirm and celebrate this with them?
- In what ways can I now release greater responsibility to them?
- What consequences from their decisions am I willing to let them experience, knowing this will have a deeper, more profound impact upon them in the long run?

5

"One of the distinctive qualities of Pro-Active Parent Coaching is that it focuses upon preparing our child for the path as opposed to preparing the path for the child."

The Power of Responsibility and the Profit of Pain

The over arching question *Pro-Active Parent Coaches* ask themselves is, "How can we best serve our children's growth in responsibility as they mature toward responsible adulthood?"

There is a conviction that transformational growth takes place through pivotal life experiences within the context of a relationship that encourages reflection and application of learning to our lives. Giving responsibility allows our children to develop their strengths, and build a reservoir of experience, from which they can draw wisdom throughout life. Reflecting upon these experiences and helping them apply learning to life, through coaching, makes this truly transformational. This is what makes the coaching relationship so powerful.

> **"We can rejoice, too, when we run into problems and trials, for we know that they help us develop endurance. And endurance develops strength of character."**
> Romans 5:3,4 (NLT)

This also communicates our care, love and concern to them in a unique way. "We love you so much that we want to prepare you as best we can for your future. Because of this, we refuse to shelter you from all pain, but commit to walking with you through it as you mature and develop in character." Sounds a little bit like God's approach with us, doesn't it?

As a parent coach we help our children reflect upon their experiences, both good and bad, then help our child leverage these for transformational growth. In the parent coaching relationship, pain can be an incredible teacher.

Controlled Pain

Controlled pain is what we allow our children to experience as a consequence of the decisions they make. Our role in parenting is to protect them from harm, not shelter them from all pain. Allowing them to experience some discomfort has a view to their future by allowing their character to be developed through these experiences, which will benefit them in the long run as adults.

> **"Giving responsibility allows our children to develop their strengths, and build a reservoir of experience from which they can draw wisdom throughout life."**

We recognize that there is 'risk' and 'faith' involved in this process. The risk is that our child may experience some pain and as parents we are supposed to be their protectors. The element of faith is recognizing that God loves our children far more than we do (as hard as this is to comprehend), and trust that He is actively at work within their lives developing the character they will need to fulfill their destiny. When we release control and give more freedom to them, we create an incredible growth environment for our children and free God to do His work within our child's life, and for a parent, this can be a very scary thing.

By way of example, I'd like to share a couple of experiences from within our own family that highlight the transformational value releasing responsibility and controlled pain have within our children's growth and development. Observe how we used coaching from a young age to strengthen our daughter's decision making ability while allowing her to experience 'controlled pain' for deeper character development.

Pro-Active Parent Coaching Opportunity

Coaching Conversation	Observation
As the heat of the summer day gave way to the coolness of the evening breeze; we sipped on refreshing glasses of iced tea. Lynn and I sat on our back deck enjoying casual conversation together when we were interrupted by the sound of skidding tires and flying gravel. Giggling and grinning ear to ear was our five year old daughter who had just come to a skidding stop beside us. Proudly sitting on her bicycle, the gleam in her eyes informed us she was 'up to something.'	At first, this may sound like a strange question from a 5 year old girl, but understand that she has already had exposure to motorcycles. They are a common part of our family life, as she began riding on the back of her Daddy's motorcycle as soon as she could touch the foot pegs.
Curiously we asked, *"What are you thinking, young lady?"* Smiling, she asked, "Mommy, Daddy, can I buy a dirt bike (motorcycle)?" Turning, I looked at Lynn and she looked back at me and smiled as only a mother can. I knew exactly what she was thinking in that moment, so I turned to Katelyn and answered, *"Sure, sweetie, you can buy a dirt bike!"* Katelyn's eyes lit up, and I continued. *"Can I ask you a couple of questions first, though?"*	Rather than shut Katelyn down by simply saying, "No. You're a bit too young for that, don't you think?" We recognized this as an opportunity for her growth in awareness and decision making. One is never too young to begin learning this so we opt to coach her in this moment by asking questions. This promotes further thought, reflection and develops her awareness.
"Sure" she said excitedly, eyes still gleaming. *"As you consider owning a dirt-bike, what do*	I encourage her by saying, "Sure," but then ask permission to explore this a bit further.

you think would be important to know even before purchasing one?"

Pausing for a moment she looked down at her bicycle, then looked back at Lynn and myself and replied, "Well, maybe, I should know how to ride this bike without the training wheels on."

"Yes, that would be a great start. Is there anything else you can think of?"

"Umm, that you guys would let me?"

"Yes, that would be good to know as well."

"Can I?"

"Can you what?"

"Can I get a dirt-bike?"

Again glancing toward Lynn for her affirmation, I then turned back to Katelyn and said, *"Of course you can, as long as certain conditions are met."*

"Cool!" – pause - "What is a condition?"

"Well, conditions are certain things that need to be taken care of before you can do something, like purchase a dirt bike, for example. You have already mentioned a couple of conditions."

"I have?"

"Yes, learning to ride a bicycle without training wheels is a very wise condition to have in place before buying a motocross bike, and of course if Mommy and Daddy agree, that's also a condition."

Pausing for a moment I let her consider what was spoken, then continued. *"Do you understand what I mean?"*

"I think so. There are some things that need to happen before I can get a dirt bike, right?"

"You got it, so lets talk about that a little bit more. You've mentioned learning to ride your bicycle without training wheels, having permission from Mommy and myself. What other things do you think need to happen before you get a dirt bike?"

"Ummmmm, money?"

"Yes that's something you will definitely need. So how much do you think you'll need to buy one?"

"I don't know how much they cost, can you tell me?"

"No, honestly I can't, because I haven't been looking for one, but I can help you pick one out and then see how much they do cost if you like?"

"Really? That's cool; I would like that a lot."

The next few weeks become an incredible

Here I move toward raising her awareness by asking her to consider what she needs to think about as opposed to simply telling her. She thinks and begins to make connections.

I continue asking to see what else we can draw out of her.

Again, rather than simply say no, I answer but state that there would need to be certain conditions met. This keeps her heart open to the possibility but establishes healthy parameters for her.

I simply explain what a 'condition' is and remain silent for a few moments as she thinks about this concept. In time I ask to ensure that she understands what I mean.

Continuing to probe by asking, "what else . . .?" "What other things . . .?"

Here's a biggie. The money factor. Katelyn doesn't know how much one will cost, which then takes this to the next level. Rather than simply saying, "I'll find out for you," I offer to help her research which keeps responsibility with Katelyn.

relationship building time for us. First, Katelyn asked if her training wheels could be removed so she could practice riding on two wheels. Daddy quickly removed the training wheels, Lynn pulled the video camera from storage and we began our adventure.

Together, Katelyn and I looked at what savings she had and talked as a family about what Mommy and Daddy would be willing to let her spend on a dirt bike. When this was determined, we spent time together researching different models and what would best serve Katelyn as she learns to ride, and what may have the best resale value in the event she doesn't enjoy it and wants to sell.

On our next family day we visited a local motorcycle dealer who allowed Katelyn to sit upon the selected model to see how it 'felt.' She quickly informed us that she 'loved the feel of this one' and her excitement soared to a new level. We opted to purchase a 'previously used' dirt bike in order to save money and designed a savings chart for Katelyn which we placed upon the refrigerator.

Within the week Katelyn was proudly navigating obstacles on our yard on two wheels without any assistance and exclaimed with excitement, "Daddy, I've got this down! How long do you think it'll take me to save up for the dirt bike?"

Smiling, I simply said, "That's a very good question, honey; let's take some time to consider that."

Recognizing her weekly allowance would not produce the money she needed quickly enough, she devised an ingenious fund raising plan that would soon be put into action. Christmas was only a few months away and true to form, family began calling asking if there was something special she would like for Christmas this year. As Katelyn talked on the phone we would hear something like, "I'm saving up for a dirt-bike, so you don't have to get me presents this year; if you like, you can just give me money so I can put it toward that."

Christmas day arrived and Katelyn felt a slight sting of pain when she noticed there were fewer wrapped gifts under the tree for her compared to our other daughter, Hannah. Instead, there were a couple of cards with her name on them nestled

This whole research process lent itself naturally to a relational connection that we still fondly look back upon.

The key for Katelyn's growth here was seen in the fact we involved her throughout the process. We could have easily done all of the work for her, or simply made the decision for her ourselves. Choosing to coach *Supported Katelyn's Growth* through this experience.

Here we have a very simple reminder that coaching has the ability to draw out the best in people. We simply coached Katelyn, and she *Explored the Possibilities*, creating her own action plan for acquiring the money she needed. We were astounded at her creativity and resourcefulness. This taught us an incredible lesson: *our children are often more capable than we give them credit for*.

amongst the tree branches. She anxiously waited for us to hand her the envelopes so she could tear into them in hopes of seeing some, cold hard cash! Ripping into the envelopes, her eyes widened and a smile broke upon her face as she held some money high and said, "Look Dad, dirt bike money!"

Although the pain she experienced that Christmas morning without tangible gifts in hand was real, it was slightly overshadowed at the prospect of being closer to purchasing her dirt bike. Unknown to all of us that Christmas morning, was that within just a few short weeks, we would have another coaching opportunity with Katelyn involving controlled pain.

The Profit of Pain

It sat innocently upon the shelf, but it still caught Katelyn's eye and tugged at her heart strings. "It's so soft, cute and cuddly; can I get it?"

Gently taking the bear from her hands I affirmed, *"You're right; it is soft, cute and cuddly,"* and handed it to Mommy so she could see too.

"Can I get it?"

"What about the dirt bike you're saving for?" I asked.

"Oh, I still want that too! But I really like this bear, it's perfect!"

"Hmmm. Are you willing to buy it with your own money? You did get a fair amount for Christmas!"

Looking at me and nodding her head, "Yes I am. I'll pay for it myself!"

"OK, can we think about this for a moment? Do you realize that when you buy this, it will take money out of your savings?"

"Yes, Daddy, I know that."

"Do you understand what that means?"

"Well, I will have to spend my own money to get the bear."

"Yes, and?"

"It will take some of my dirt bike money to do it."

"Do you know what that means in the long run?"

"No, I am not sure."

"OK, do you mind if I explain it to you?"

"Please."

"If you take money from your dirt bike savings,

I quickly became aware of the potential for a growth opportunity regarding financial management. Knowing that Katelyn is saving for the dirt bike I simply want to draw this to her attention, and also ask if she would be willing to use her own money.

Allowing her to make the decision keeps responsibility with Katelyn and brings greater impact to the learning. She will either consider it and decide not to purchase the toy, feeling a slight sting of pain in that way. Or, she will buy it and experience the pain associated with spending some of her own savings. In my mind it is a 'low cost' learning opportunity and will be great learning experience while she is young.

I ask to ensure that she understands the long term consequences of her decision. It's important that she not only makes the decision herself, but makes an informed decision. In addition to this, I want to help her *that will leave less there. Which means to build it back up again, it will take longer to do so. Do you understand that?"*

"Yes Daddy. I know, and that's OK. I really want this bear."

"OK, I just wanted to make sure that you understand. The choice is yours, sweetie, but before you make your final decision, would you be willing to take a little more time to think about it?"

"OK," she said with a distinctly disappointed tone.

"Here is my suggestion: we'll put this back on the shelf and you think about it while we continue shopping. If you still want it and are willing to buy it yourself when we finish, you can. The choice is yours!"

With a big smile she took the bear from my hands, "OK, thanks Daddy," and gently placed it upon the shelf with a kind pat on the head.

As we concluded shopping and began toward the checkouts, I knelt down and whispered softly in Katelyn's ear, *"Have you decided what you want to do about the bear, sweetie?"*

"Yes, Daddy, I did."

"What are you going to do?"

"I really, really, want it, so I'm going to buy it."

"You're positive?"

"Yes."

"OK, go get it and you can buy it."

Katelyn quickly ran to the shelf and gently lifted the bear from where it was placed an hour before. Grinning from ear to ear she walked toward us at the checkouts and said, "You'll like our house, it's a real nice place to live."

Arriving home, we unloaded the van and then gathered in the kitchen, *"One last thing to do, sweetie,"* I said as I took her savings chart off of the refrigerator.

She smiled and held her new friend as we subtracted the price of the bear from her savings toward the dirt bike, and placed it back upon the refrigerator.

A couple of weeks later I was sitting reading in the family room and Katelyn came, nestled onto my lap and said, "Daddy, I wish I didn't buy that bear."

"Really?" I said, "I thought you loved that bear!

learn self control and avoid being an impulse buyer. So I affirm she has the final decision, but ask for her to take a little more time to think about it.

In order to prevent 'impulse buying' tendencies, I suggest taking time to think about the purchase then make the final decision.

I honor Katelyn here, by keeping responsibility for the decision with her. Allowing her the freedom to make this decision and not over-ruling her by saying no. In this moment I am choosing to allow experience to be her teacher and trust that in time, she will learn the valuable lesson this opportunity can bring her.

In order for the lesson to have influence upon Katelyn, I cannot shelter her from it. It would have been easy to say, "I've been thinking, the bear was only a few dollars, forget about it and I'll give it to you as a gift." Doing this would not have taught Katelyn responsibility or good financial stewardship.

We allow experience to be the teacher and refrain from saying something like, "I told you so." Or, "If you would have listened to me, …" To do so

What makes you say that?"

"Well, now I have to save up longer to buy my dirt bike."

"Yes, that is true; it will take a bit longer."

"Yeah."

"How does that make you feel?"

"I don't feel so good about it now."

"No?"

"No, I have other stuffed animals, and didn't really need another one, and I was saving toward the dirt bike and now have less money for it."

"Yeah, I haven't liked those feelings either when I've made similar decisions."

"You've done this before?"

"Yes, honey, I have. I've learned a lot about finances from some painful decisions that I have made growing up."

"It's not nice, is it?"

"No, it doesn't feel good inside at the time, but, there is a lot we can learn through these experiences. If you could do this over again, what would you do differently?"

"I would just leave the bear there and save the money!" she stated emphatically.

Smiling I gave her a big hug and affirmed, *"It's OK sweetie, I think you have learned a valuable lesson about money and saving through this, which will help you become a very wise young lady! Don't worry, it may take a bit longer, but one day you will have enough to buy a dirt bike."*

would strip the experience of its power. Instead, I simply ask, "What makes you say that?" and allow her to share what she is thinking, and learning, through this experience.

I empathize with her by letting her know I've made similar decisions and felt that pain too.

For the lesson to hit home, I want her to consider now what she would do differently when facing a similar situation.

I conclude by affirming that what she has learned will help make her a wise young lady and she will one day have enough to purchase the dirt-bike. Inside I am rejoicing, knowing that this painful experience has become a valuable learning experience for her.

Coaching our children from a young age can be an incredibly rewarding and life shaping experience for both us and our children. This experience had a profound impact upon our family. It helped us connect relationally by: Intentionally taking time together, allowing Katelyn to make decisions and grow in her ability to do so, and encouraging transparency between one another in conversation.

Lynn and I marveled at how resourceful a young child could be, which strengthened our understanding of how capable children can be, and our commitment to coaching all of our children as they would respond to it. The greatest moment in all of this, for me, came one month after Katelyn's 6th birthday, when she had enough money saved to make her purchase. We took time together searching used motorcycle ads and located a dirt bike for her to purchase. Nothing could beat that wide smile and the incredible sense of accomplishment that Katelyn had when she sat upon that bike for the first time.

"Coaching our children from a young age can be an incredibly rewarding and life shaping experience for both us and our children."

Pictured here is Katelyn, in her safety gear, on the day she purchased her dirt bike.

"When we release control and give more freedom to our children, we create an incredible growth environment for them."

Concluding that story may leave some of you thinking, "Are you two crazy?" and others wondering, "What was the recognizable long term impact this experience had upon Katelyn?"

Those are both good questions and I'll begin by entertaining the former. It has been in our heart to foster a home environment that is Pro-Active in our children's development, knowing that one day they will leave the shelter of our home and continue following the path that God has ordained for them. Although that may seem like a long way off, you and I both know that years go by quickly, and before we know it, they are young adults leaving home.

In light of this truth, we made a commitment to making the most of every opportunity to prepare our children for responsible adulthood. Coaching would take a very prominent place within our parenting. We asked ourselves, "What skills and life experience will best serve our children as they launch out from our home?" Then we began relating to them in terms of their future as responsible adults, and giving freedom to make decisions and take responsibility that is in keeping with their natural ability. In this way, we provide them with the necessary experience from which they can draw wisdom later in life.

In our minds, all of this is best done within the context of a loving and restorative home environment through which they can reflect upon their experience and apply learning to life.

But a motorcycle? Yes, a motorcycle. This was her dream, and we wanted to foster an environment that could help her dream become a reality in the safest way possible. We ensured that Katelyn had all the safety equipment necessary, and to top it off I had the privilege of spending additional time teaching her how to ride. This served to strengthen our relational bonds even more. Although the dirt-bike is pretty quick, it had a speed limiter installed which allowed me to increase her speed as her ability increased.

Having the dirt bike allowed us to teach two additional values to Katelyn, and subsequently our other children. 1. Falling is a natural part of learning, and 2. People hold greater value than things. We affirmed over and over when one would have an accident, "Don't worry about the bike, it's just a *thing*, and it's replaceable! How are you?"

This was truly an invaluable experience for Katelyn and for us as parents. Giving her the freedom to make these decisions, and stepping back, allowing her to experience the consequences, 'controlled pain,' has had an incredible impact upon her life. She, as our other children, have grown in awareness and developed a greater ability to reflect before committing to a course of action.

This now leads us to the second question,

> "What is the recognizable long term impact this experience had upon Katelyn?"

Rather than simply tell you what we see, I'd like to allow you to observe the difference coaching has made within her life through these experiences, by observing a more recent coaching conversation with Katelyn about a decision she wanted to make.

As you read through the following conversation, keep in mind that six years have passed between the previously discussed experience and this conversation. Try to identify areas in which Katelyn shows evidence of being shaped by her previous experience. Also, take note of how we as parents maintain a coaching posture and work in cooperation with her ability so that she can continue growing in maturity, by taking responsibility for her decision and actions.

Pro-Active Parent Coaching Opportunity

Coaching Conversation	Observation

Sometime after the children were 'sleeping,' the sound of stairs creaking underfoot caught our attention. As the sound of footsteps made their way across the floor overhead toward the stairway we listened carefully trying to guess which child this was. Looking toward the stairwell, we saw one foot, then another appear and hesitate on the top step as if to ask, "Is it OK to come down?"
    Recognizing it was Katelyn we affirmed, *"It's OK Katelyn, come on down. Are you having trouble sleeping?"*
    "Yeah," she said somberly, continuing to the fourth step before sitting and peering at us with those big green eyes.
    "What's on your mind?"
    "Mom, Dad, I have made a decision that I'd like to talk to you about."
    "OK, what is it?"	

"You know how I want to buy a horse, right?"

"*Yes.*" (Realistically, there is no way we could forget: pictures, screen-savers, notebooks, talk, talk and more talk.)

"But I am also taking horse riding lessons."

"*Yes.*"

"I've been doing some math, and because my lessons cost $25.00 each, what I have saved toward buying a horse would be used up in just 32 lessons."

"*OK.*"

"So what I was thinking is this: it might be better if I stopped taking lessons and continued to save up to buy a horse instead, and then I could learn to ride and stuff with my own horse. What do you think of that idea?"

"*Is that something you really want to do?*"

"I think so."

"*Can I ask another question?*"

"Sure."

"*Is your mind already made up or are you still thinking about it?*"

"Well, . . . I am still thinking it through, but wanted to talk with you guys about it. But I was also thinking, if I saved up and bought a horse, learned to ride well on my own, then I could teach others and charge them $25.00 per lesson. That way I am making money at the same time."

"*That's very true. I like the way you think. What can we do to help you with this decision?*"

"We can talk more about it."

"*Sure, we'd love to, but right now you should get some rest, so when would you like to talk about it?*"

"How about on our next date?"

With a laugh, "*OK, that's sounds great to me; we'll talk about it then. You can put it out of your mind and go on back to bed and get a good rest.*"

"OK, thank you." Standing and beginning to walk up the stairs, she turns one last time to say, "Good night, I'll see you in the morning!"

Date Day

Katelyn and I sat on the park bench feeding the ducks. For some time I simply sat sipping my iced tea and watched Katelyn fiddle with her hot chocolate. She was obviously caught up in

Katelyn has stated her desire to purchase a horse, but also shares that she's been doing some math. She has worked out how much her riding lessons cost and what that is doing to her savings toward the purchase of a horse. This shows us that she has grown in her awareness of decisions and managing money.

Katelyn shows that she has already begun *Exploring Possibilities* on her own.

I ask to *Assess her Desire* and commitment to the decision. Her response, "I think so," indicates that she may still be struggling with the decision. I ask permission to ask a further question to help me assess her desire and gain an understanding of how committed she is to this.

She opens up and shares more which helps us understand what she is thinking. Katelyn is really still *Exploring Possibilities* and hasn't secured a commitment to a specific action step.

Affirm her thought processes, and ask how she would like us to help her. This gives her an opportunity to tell us exactly how she would like us to function and support her during this time.

She asks to talk about this more and sets a time to do so.

Katelyn was obviously deep in thought, so I took the opportunity to re-engage our conversation so I can understand what she is thinking.

her own thoughts so I re-engaged our previous conversation about riding lessons.

"Well Katelyn, it looks like you're doing some serious thinking. Can you tell me more about your thoughts regarding riding lessons?"

"I've been thinking about it a lot lately. I know stopping the lessons would help me save my money and I'd be able to buy a horse sooner, but it kind of hurts at the same time when I think about not taking them."

"That's interesting; tell me more about that."

"Well, I really like horses."

Chuckling, I replied teasingly, *"Really? I am not sure I would have guessed that about you!"*

"Come on Dad, you know me better than that. I know I'd miss Robyn (the horse), and Danielle (the teacher); that makes me kind of sad because I really like them and she is such a nice teacher."

- Long Pause -

" The lessons really would help me to learn better and I still want to have a farm when I grow up. So this will give me more experience with horses, taking care of them, grooming them, and yeah, that kind of stuff."

- Pause -

"Plus I'd be more comfortable around horses when I get my own. You know, maybe it would be better for me to keep doing some lessons and not stop them completely right now."

"That is definitely an option. Talk a little more about that as a possibility."

"Well, lessons would actually help me to learn better and faster than if I tried to learn on my own."

"True enough."

"I think that it would be good as well, if I have more experience before I buy a horse. That way I can be a lot more comfortable on and around them."

- Pause -

"Maybe, I'd even be able to offer kids lessons sooner because of what I will have learned! What do you think Dad?"

Rather than jump to conclusions about what, "It kind of hurts," might mean, I simply ask her to tell me about it. This gives her opportunity to share more information which will help me understand what she is thinking and feeling.

As Katelyn shares what she is thinking there are moments when she simply grows quiet. It's fairly easy to tell that she is doing some serious thinking and it's a bit emotional for her.

I refrain from interrupting her thoughts with questions or comments and allow her to fully process and articulate what she is thinking and feeling.

As a side note, I love what I am hearing as a Dad. She is truly thinking through this decision and considering many angles to it. I transition to *Supporting Growth* now as I ask her to tell me more about this possibility.

Notice that as she talks there is a growing awareness that she really wants to continue with her riding lessons as opposed to quitting them.

"Well, I think those are great thoughts, when you think about continuing your lessons, is there anything else that comes to mind?"

"Honestly, I really do like taking horse riding lessons."

"Yeah, Mom and I can tell, and you look like a natural. No doubt this has been a hard decision for you to consider. So, as you think about both possibilities, quitting or continuing, which is more appealing to you?"

"Well, I think I'm changing my mind, and would like to continue taking them. Is that OK?"

"Absolutely, Mom and I would support whichever decision you made."

"What do you think of all of this, Dad?"

"First, I appreciate your openness to talk about these things. I know they are important to you and that means a lot to me, as your Dad. From my perspective, Katelyn, it looks to me as though you are thinking things through really well. You're considering different angles, and weighing out the pros and cons of this decision. If I understand you correctly, it seems to me like you are at a place of decision. Do I stop taking lessons and save my money to buy a horse, or do I continue lessons and increase my horsemanship?"

"Yeah, that's where I am, alright."

"So, I'll ask my question again: which are you leaning toward, stopping the lessons or continuing?"

"Well, I think I'm leaning toward continuing my lessons."

"You think?"

Katelyn laughs, "Yeah, I THINK I'll do that."

"That doesn't sound very convincing to me. Is that really what you want to do?"

Katelyn gives her familiar laugh, "Yeah, I'm sure."

"So, how are you going to proceed from here?"

"I'll keep taking my lessons and learning to ride the horse. Maybe I can offer to do chores and stuff in exchange for lessons and that will help me save money too."

"Excellent idea! So how can we support you through this time?"

"Just keep doing what you're doing Dad. I appreciate the fact we can talk about these things."

"That I can do. I love watching you grow and

Keep responsibility with her by refraining from offering my advice or telling her what to do and simply *asking* and *listening* as she continues thinking about these possibilities.

Affirmation of her ability here and the fact this is not an easy decision for her.

I'm *Assessing Desire* now by asking her to consider both possibilities and tell me which is more appealing to her.

Affirm its 'OK' to change her mind and select a different course of action. This highlights that she is in control of the decision and we will support her with whichever she chooses.

I thank her for being open which affirms our family value of transparency. Then simply proceed to telling her what I see as she has wrestled through this decision, and summarize to ensure I understand what she is thinking.

She affirms I do understand correctly where she is within the decision making process and I keep responsibility with her by asking which decision she is leaning toward.

Katelyn knows the coaching process pretty well and expects me to *Secure Commitment*, so she jokingly emphasizes, *"I think,"* at this point.

I *Secure Commitment* by asking how she is going to proceed from here. I could have asked, "What are you going to do now?" "What is your plan?" "What is your action step?" When telling me what she is going to do, she thinks of another possibility: doing chores in exchange for riding lessons. Concluding, I ask how we can continue supporting her through this.

mature in these areas. It's one of the privileges of being a parent. Katelyn, can I share something with you now that your decision is made?"

"Yeah, that's not a problem."

"Well, Mommy and Daddy are very proud of you and are excited to see who you are becoming as a person. In light of this, we already talked about your decision the other night and came to a decision of our own."

"Oh, what's that?"

"Well, we felt that the horse riding lessons have been very good for you and we're excited to see what God continues to do in your heart through them. So, we have decided to help you out some with your lessons, as an investment in your future."

"Really? That's awesome, Dad! You know I don't expect that, right?"

"Yes, both Mom and I know that you don't expect it, but we also wanted to be a blessing to you, and this is one way we can do that."

"Thanks, that means a lot to me."

Verbally I *Encourage her Progress.*

By holding onto this information until she had completely come to a decision allowed the process to have its full effect within her. This allowed her to continue in her development and growth with decision making and taking responsibility. Additionally it brought great encouragement to her by offering support beyond what she expected.

Reflection

- In what ways did you see Katelyn's previous experience shaping her current thoughts?
- How did we, as parents, keep responsibility with Katelyn?
- What examples in the conversation did you see that kept responsibility with Katelyn, as opposed to removing it from her?
- What is one thing that you noticed about coaching here that you could begin implementing within your own parenting right away?

One of the distinctive qualities of *Pro-Active Parent Coaching* is that it focuses upon preparing our child for the path as opposed to preparing the path for the child. This allows them the opportunity to gain experience from which to draw wisdom as they mature and will greatly increase their success at navigating life beyond the shelter of our homes. In this way we are displaying the depth of our love for them, evidenced by our willingness to release control, give responsibility and allow them to experience some pain along the way. At the same time we are offering the support and encouragement they need as they mature toward responsible adulthood.

You now understand what *Pro-Active Parent Coaching* is and how it helps us cooperate with our children's *Natural Growth Patterns*. Are you ready to dive into the *Pro-Active Parent Coaching* Model? If so, let's continue on to Part 2, where we will gain a greater understanding of, and practice, the heart, skills, and disciplines of *Pro-Active Parent Coaching.*

Chapter

6

Part 2
Supporting Relationship through Understanding

> "Jumping to
> conclusions is the only
> exercise some people
> get."

A good friend Phil and I were talking about misunderstandings, when he began to laugh. After I asked what prompted his laughter, he shared the following story.

> "Fear gripped my heart like a vice as the four dreaded words, 'Dad, what's a condom?' left my 11-year-old boy's lips. My face flushed and I felt my blood pressure rise almost immediately. 'Where in the world did this come from? How did our pleasant afternoon walk suddenly swing in this direction?' Pausing for a moment, I held my gaze out across the meadow. Avoiding eye contact with my son I hoped to mask my discomfort with his question. After what seemed like minutes, I broke the silence and began explaining to my son James about the 'birds and the bees.'
>
> James listened intently as I explained the wonderful complexity of human life and the sexuality that God had fashioned within us. I emphasized the fact that we are fearfully and wonderfully made, explaining that his body was changing, and he would begin sensing and feeling things that would be very new to him.
>
> Seconds turned to minutes, and the minutes seemed like an eternity. Already mentally exhausted, my mind raced with all the changes my son was beginning to experience. Puberty, girls, attraction, peer pressure, sexuality, temptation, STD's; where would all of this lead? Would he understand? Could I prepare him to be the godly man that he should be?
>
> I wanted to instill within him knowledge of the awesome gift that God had given us in sexuality and at the same time encourage him to save this gift for his life time partner. If I had known this conversation was going to take place on this day, I would have taken time to prepare myself!
>
> Pausing once more to collect my thoughts and carefully craft my next words, I summoned up the courage to speak, but my son broke the silence first. His shy voice

indicated he was noticeably confused and he said, 'Oh, I had heard that they were building some condoms here in the field next summer.'"

Phil wiped tears of laughter from his eyes as he confessed, "Greg, you know that moment in the field with James taught me an incredible lesson. I have learned to ask questions, and listen carefully, so that I can understand before jumping to conclusions and running off at the mouth."

"He who answers before listening— that is his folly and his shame."
Proverbs 18:13 (NIV)

I nodded in agreement, trying to restrain my own laughter and responded, "I agree and I couldn't think of a better or more humorous way to have learned this."

My friend Phil was very transparent that day and I know many of us could share similar, if not more embarrassing stories of how we jumped to conclusions, believing we understood what the speaker was saying only to discover afterward that we were on an entirely different page. These often humorous moments can serve as incredible reminders for us, indicating that we do not always understand what someone is really thinking.

Reflection

Recall a recent conversation with your child in which you jumped to conclusions and began giving your thoughts and opinions, only to discover later that you completely misunderstood what your child intended.

- How did that experience affect your child?
- When you realized you misunderstood, how did that affect you personally?
- What mental notes did you make?
- What changes, if any, did you resolve to make as a result of that experience?
- How has that experience changed your approach to others in conversation?

As you consider how your child views your understanding of them, what do you believe, at this moment, your child would say about you as a parent?

Fill in the blank
My Mom/Dad, _____ understand me.
(Always, sometimes, never, seldom, doesn't care to, seeks to, tries to, loves to, ... other descriptors?)

James' father Phillip, in the above story, hit the proverbial nail on the head, "I have learned to ask questions and listen carefully so that I can understand before jumping to conclusions and running off at the mouth." Although it's a humorous and powerful way to learn this lesson, understanding serves a greater purpose than simply keeping us out of embarrassing situations. It communicates great respect for our children and is foundational to healthy relationships. It's important to note in parenting, that far too often misunderstandings are the fuel for relational conflict.

Consider the following quote on understanding:

> "I have found it of enormous value when I can permit myself to understand the other person. The way in which I have worded this statement may seem strange to you. Is it necessary to permit oneself to understand another? I think it is. Our first reaction to most of the statements (which we hear from other people) is an evaluation or judgment, rather than an understanding of it. When someone expresses some feeling, attitude or belief, our tendency is almost immediately to feel "that's right," or "that's stupid," "that's abnormal," "that's unreasonable," " that's incorrect," "that's not nice." Very rarely do we permit ourselves to understand precisely what the meaning of the statement is to the other person."[3]

Understanding, in the broad sense of the term, is an intimate knowledge of our children discovered through the continued relationship we share with them. In other words, we have a growing understanding of what God is forming within them, and who they are becoming. They are unique and different from anyone else; possessing different gifts, passions, desires, fears, shortcomings, failures, longings, strengths, and callings. Anyone having more than one child will testify to the fact that although they may come from the same family and have similarities, they are tremendously unique.

"Understanding, in the broad sense of the term, is an intimate knowledge of our children discovered through the continued relationship we share with them."

Deeply seated within each of us is a longing to be known and understood. This makes understanding powerful in supporting healthy relationships. When we intentionally focus upon understanding our children, we capture their hearts by touching one of their greatest felt needs, and relationship is supported, trust is developed, and an invitation into the deeper parts of their lives naturally follows.

When we focus upon *Supporting Relationship through Understanding* it creates the environment needed to establish and maintain health within our relationship together. It supports our relationship because it brings clarity and accuracy to how we view and approach our children. Understanding has the power to:

> Change our perspective.
> Prevent us from making rash judgments.
> Re-adjust our expectations when necessary, and
> Increase our relational bonds.

In the context of communication, Webster's Dictionary defines understanding as: "To achieve a grasp of the nature, significance, or explanation of something."[4] Therefore, understanding for us as parents is a confidence that we know and grasp what our child is thinking, feeling and experiencing with no reservation or doubt lingering within our mind. In conversation, understanding has been reached when the thoughts and intentions of the heart are communicated, and understood, by both the child and parent.

This is accomplished by intentionally employing four simple disciplines within our conversations,

          Connecting
              Asking
                    Listening, and
                          Clarifying.

The following conversational model illustrates how these disciplines work together to *Support Relationship through Understanding*.

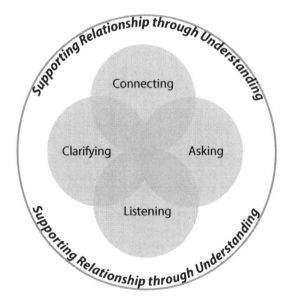

The power and beauty of the *Supporting Relationship through Understanding* Model is found within its simplicity and its intentional focus upon establishing and maintaining health within relationships. In essence we're emulating God's approach with us as His children by making relationship our first priority.

The disciplines of *Connecting, Asking, Listening,* and *Clarifying* are depicted as intersecting circles because they do not stand alone but work in harmony as they bring understanding. Although we will observe each discipline individually in a clockwise fashion, as we hone our skills we will notice the process is more fluid, moving back and forth between the elements, as we gain understanding of our children. For instance, we may discover that we begin with listening because our child has approached us and initiated conversation. We may then follow up with asking, listening more, asking again, then clarifying to ensure we have understood what they intended.

Often you will notice within a coaching conversation, the disciplines of *asking*, then *listening* without interrupting, allows deeper matters of the heart to surface. This is illustrated well in the following coaching conversation. Observe how the disciplines of *Connecting, Asking, Listening and Clarifying* work in harmony as understanding is attained through the following coaching conversation with Amy.

Coaching Conversation	Observation

"I am facing a decision and don't know what to do. I am wondering if I can get your opinion on something."

"OK, can I ask you some questions and we'll see where that takes us?"

"Sure."

"Talk about this a bit more so I can understand what decision you are facing."

"Well, I want to take a mission trip to Africa and see what God is asking me to do with my life, but on the other hand I want to attend Bible College. This has been the plan all along, but lately I have a growing burden within my heart for cross cultural work. What I am thinking is this; I'd like to take some time, go overseas and do an extended mission trip. Maybe this will help me discover what God is saying to me about this burden for cross cultural work. Where it gets difficult is I would not be able to attend college this fall as originally planned and instead I'd have to work to save up the money for the trip. That is difficult for me because the plans for college have already been made."

"I think you are in a very interesting and exciting time of your life! What do you need to know within your heart and mind in order to make this decision with confidence?"

"Honestly, I'd like to know that my parents and my pastor understand why I am going to Africa, and feel their support in this."

"Tell me about the significance of that for you."

"I would like to be in Africa and although away from family, friends and church, know that I have their support with what I am doing. If I didn't have the support and went anyway, I know it would be very distracting for me; it would be on my mind all the time and I know that isn't what God would want for my life."

- reflective pause -

"I want to be able to go over there, experience cross cultural work and really connect with what God may be saying to me about my future without that kind of baggage hanging on me. So yeah, that is why the support is significant for me."

Connection is made easily because of the relationship we already share. I've been Amy's pastor for several years and have cultivated trust between us, making it easy for her to approach me.

Asking her to share more so I understand what the decision is that she is thinking about.

Listening to gain understanding.

Asking and then giving Amy the freedom to speak brings a significant piece of information out on the table here. Conversation moves now from making a difficult decision to knowing people understand her motives for taking this trip.

Choosing to coach this situation by asking and listening in this way brought some very important information out in the open that otherwise would not have been considered.

Motive for the trip is revealed.

"That's great. From my perspective as your pastor, you have my support and the support of the church family. Can we focus upon your parents for a moment?"

"Yes, that's OK."

"What would it look like to you knowing that they support you?"

- reflective pause -

"Well, they would support me in the decision, not so much financially because that isn't what I am looking for. I just want them to know and understand why I am not going to college this fall. I will go, but I really have this burden and need to sort out what that means for my life. I know that it can seem like I am throwing away a year of my life. But, in my mind, it's only one year, and maybe God can really direct me through this. I think I'd know their support in the fact that they really understood my motives for going. It's not simply to ditch college or have a good time away from home, but to get a handle on this burden I am feeling."

"That sounds very good. Let me see if I understand correctly. It sounds like your saying that your desire is really having the knowledge that your parents understand your motives with the decision, is that correct?"

"Yes, that is the most important thing to me, that I don't just take off and they really don't understand what I am thinking or feeling or why I am doing this. It isn't just about a vacation or skipping out from school. I really am trying to determine what to do with my life and I have a great burden for those cross culturally."

I affirm my support as her pastor and ask if we can focus upon her parents.

Clarifying now to ensure I understand her correctly.

Confirmation. True understanding only comes when the individual confirms that we have understood correctly. This is a critical step which gives our children permission to correct our thinking if necessary.

Resisting the temptation to jump in too quickly, offering opinion, or making judgments has the potential to draw out of an individual some deeper thoughts and values, which is easily seen in this conversation. What initially came as a request for my opinion on a difficult decision really boiled down to Amy's desire to be understood by her parents. What came to the surface was a deeper value she holds, the value of having her parents support, through understanding her motives. Amy is honestly seeking to discover what God is forming within her and not simply looking to waste a year of her life on an expensive trip. Coaching in this way brought a deeper value to the surface and opened the door to naturally transition to *Supporting her Growth*.

We continued our coaching conversation with me asking, "What is the best way for your parents to truly understand your motives?" This turned Amy's mind toward *Exploring this Possibility, Assessing her Desire* to move forward and *Securing a Commitment* to speaking openly with her parents within the following two days.

She followed through with her commitment; her parents gained an understanding of her motives and gave her the support she needed. After saving enough money, she had the privilege of spending several months overseas where she gained a greater understanding of what God was doing within her life. Returning to Canada she enrolled in cross cultural studies at Bible College where she is currently studying.

The impact of coaching is incredible. It brought a deeper value to the surface for Amy to reflect on, helped her connect with what God was doing in her life, and begin taking steps toward its fulfillment.

> **"Coaching is something that really hit me, and was a benefit to me. I think it would be almost revolutionary if parents began using it."**
> Amy Warnock

How did Amy respond to this coaching experience? Let's hear from Amy herself.

Amy's Response to Coaching

"To be very honest- it really struck me when my pastor coached me. I was a little bit stressed, and was just expecting a lot of advice and ideas. Advice and ideas are good things, especially from someone with more life experience and knowledge than me; however, when I sat down and told him what I was thinking, instead of me doing the listening, he simply got my mind going and waited for me to talk. I was very struck by this and appreciated it a lot."

"I personally found coaching to be a very effective way to help me make my own decision. I got to sit down with someone I respect, and who has more life experience than me—and instead of telling me what they think I should do, they used their own wisdom and knowledge to guide me through questions that I should consider. I never even thought about some of the things my pastor asked me, and it genuinely helped me feel confident in the decision I was worrying about. If I could encourage people taking the coaching course, I would say that I genuinely found it a lot more beneficial to be guided through making my own decision, instead of being told what someone thought was the best for me. It was very encouraging and very helpful."

"I think that younger people need to have times to sit at the feet of those older than them, but coaching is something that really hit me, and was a benefit to me. I think it would be almost revolutionary if parents began using it. It would help us to make the best decision, and understand why we are making that decision."

Throughout the next four chapters we will look at each discipline within the *Supporting Relationship through Understanding* model individually. After that, we will put all the elements together and model for you their use and effectiveness in coaching our children. As you practice these disciplines within your own parenting, enjoy the journey into Understanding!

Chapter 7

Connecting

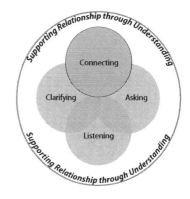

Parents struggling with their transition from telling to coaching have often made similar statements. 'Is it possible to engage in heartfelt conversation with our children if we have not experienced it up to this point?' 'Will coaching help me?' 'Is it too late to begin?' These are great questions to ask, and the good news is, engaging in a thoughtful coaching conversation with your child is possible, but it will take patience, effort and intentionality.

For parents new to coaching the bigger question is, "Where should we focus our time and energy; on asking a great question, or in establishing a healthy relationship?" It doesn't matter how good our questions are, if we do not have a relational connection, the answer we receive may lack meaning, heart, and depth, failing to lead us into the meaningful coaching conversation we had hoped for. It is not simply a powerful question that brings depth and health to our relationship; rather, it's the depth and health of our relationship that gives the question its power. That is why a relational connection is the first priority and focus within the *Pro-Active Parent Coaching* Model.

Connecting is a fundamental element of *Supporting Relationship through Understanding*. It opens the door to heartfelt conversation and is a supporting element to gain an understanding of our children. It is important to know that moments of connection cannot be fabricated, demanded or conjured up at will; rather they take place most naturally within the normal rhythms of family life. This being said, do not wait for

> **"It doesn't matter how good our questions are, if we do not have a relational connection, the answer we receive may lack meaning, heart and depth."**

chance meetings with your children hoping for a genuine heartfelt conversation; it probably won't happen. Rather, be intentional about creating an environment in which these moments of connection are not only natural but common.

"It is not simply a powerful question that brings depth and health to our relationship; rather, it's the depth and health of our relationship that gives the question its power."

Connecting with our children takes place naturally within an environment of relational closeness. In general, people will not open their hearts to another if they do not feel close to or trust them. In other words, there needs to be a relational connection. Our children are no different. Simply living in the same house does not make this relational connection automatic, which we know all too well. A relational connection must be cultivated and the best way to achieve this is through frequent shared experiences. These shared experiences serve to support relational closeness with one another making moments of connection both natural and normal.

As I sit and reflect upon this chapter, a recent family hike stands out in my mind which illustrates this point very well. Hiking has become one of our regular family activities, giving us an opportunity to enjoy the outdoors but more importantly time together as a family. The hike that stands out in my mind took us on a several kilometer journey through forest and eventually broke out onto the Atlantic coastline providing tremendous views of the ocean.

As we meandered along the forest trail, our oldest daughter walked up close beside me and asked, "Dad, can you tell me about what attracted you to Mom when you first met?" What a great question, I thought to myself, as I began to answer her. That one question gave us an opportunity to openly talk together about character, love, and commitment through very difficult circumstances. She listened, asked questions, and soon began sharing about the characteristics she would value in her future husband. What did we see along the forest trail that day? I honestly don't know. What I do know is this: as we talked we enjoyed much more than a casual conversation - it was much richer and more meaningful. In that moment we experienced a true connection.

What made this connection possible? There are four common elements we have recognized that make these moments of connection not only possible, but probable. *Consistency, Availability, Relevancy, and Transparency*, I've fondly dubbed these the *C.A.R.T.* principle of *connecting*.

What I personally love about this whole process is the fact that anyone can do it. We do not need a degree in child psychology, we do not have to be the perfect parent or do everything right to foster an environment of connection with our children. Anyone can begin *Supporting Relationship* by creating frequently shared experiences which will lend themselves most naturally to moments of connection.

Our children are longing for connection, but, just as we do, they need a sense of security within the relationship to truly open their hearts to us. In effect they are saying, "When I feel secure and know that I can trust you, I will open up and give you permission to touch the deeper areas of my life." The good news is, creating this environment is within our grasp and begins by cultivating an environment of trust based upon these four critical elements, *Consistency, Availability, Relevancy, and Transparency.*

Consistency

Structuring and committing time to regular activities in family life for the purpose of *Supporting Relationship* is a great way to foster an environment through which *Connecting* is natural and normal. *Consistency* does something unique within the hearts of our children. Within a very unstable world it brings a sense of stability by giving them something they can count on and look forward to.

Consistency also brings the priority of relationship into sharp focus, modeling for our children the value we place on relationships over things. When our children see, know and understand that we value our relationship together it gives greater credibility to me as a parent when I say, "I love you," "I'll be here for you when you need me," or "How can I support you during this time?" which otherwise might ring hollow.

The key with *consistency* is working diligently with our families in establishing a regular rhythm that fits the unique characteristics of our family unit. What works well for one family may not work for another. Once the plan is established there must be a commitment to follow through, or alter the plan as necessary as opposed to simply abandoning it.

As our own children have matured over the years we have recognized that our shared experiences have changed significantly and we have involved them more in the planning of our family times together.

Even though every moment we share together as a family may not result in that deep, heartfelt conversation, we are still strengthening relational bonds through which those moments of connection become not only possible but probable.

Availability

> "I am not sure I remember a time when my Dad and I had a good relationship. He always comes to me asking, 'Why won't you talk?' 'Why won't you open up?' He even keeps insisting, 'I'm here for you anytime you need me, just ask.' But when I come to him he is always preoccupied or busy with one of the 'many important things he deals with.' Sure he promises he'll talk later, but later never seems to come. You know, I know Dad is busy and has important things to do, but how come when his friends call or pop over saying they need him, he immediately drops everything to help them?"
> Roberta, 15

One of the more important questions our children ask is, "Will you be there when I need you?" Although there are times we feel as though they are simply tolerating us, they honestly want a healthy relationship with us that brings the security of knowing we will be available for them when they need us.

> **"In a world of uncertainty, one of the greatest assurances we can give our children is our availability to them - to be there when they need us."**

Simply put, the best time and place to connect with our children is when they approach us and ask us to. "Hey Dad, do you want to come outside and play catch?" "Mom, can we chat for a minute?" "I've been thinking about something and would like to talk." "I really need you right now!" Words like this often come at inopportune times and may appear more like an intrusion for us than an invitation into their life. Making ourselves available at these times is critical for *Connecting*, but our children are looking for more than just our physical presence. They want us to connect with, understand, and know who they really are; what they are thinking, feeling, and experiencing, all of which takes time and undivided attention. Our children are perceptive enough to know when we are giving them focussed attention, or are simply there 'in body' but not in mind.

Invitations inviting us into their world may come more frequently than we realize. Can I challenge you to be aware of these invitations throughout your days? They can be incredible moments of connection when we make ourselves available by saying something like, "I'd love to, just give me a moment to finish up so I can give you my undivided attention."

In a world of uncertainty, one of the greatest assurances we can give our children is our availability to them - to be there when they need us. As a husband, Dad, pastor and community volunteer, I understand how busy life can be and the many calls for our attention we experience throughout the day. Although there are many times my child asks for my undivided attention when I can set aside what I am currently doing and give it to them, there are those rare occasions in which I legitimately cannot do so. What do I do in these moments? How can I affirm my support of them when I cannot be there during those times?

These are great questions, that at one time or another all parents have probably struggled with. How do I draw a balance here, assuring my child that I am available when they need me but remain connected with what I am doing at the moment when necessary? A friend shared the following story with me about how he handled this situation in their family.

> Our desire is to be available right when our children need us, but as you and I both know, there are times when it is near impossible to do so. This created a tension within Sarah and I as we thought about the insecurity that so many children live with day to day. We just knew it was our responsibility to bring a greater sense of security to our own children.
>
> When we first sat down with our children and made a commitment to be there for them when they needed us, they looked genuinely relieved. As I continued explaining that there would probably be times that they would request our attention but we may not be immediately available for them, this stirred immediate concern within them. Our oldest asked, 'What if I really, really need you and you're busy with this or that, what then? What happens to me as I wait for you to be done what you're doing?'

'Those are good questions! Mom and I have been struggling with them ourselves,' I affirmed, "and we are hoping that together we can come up with a reasonable solution to that tonight.' With that said, we sat as a family around our coffee table and devised the following plan. Our family loves football, so we made it fun by building our plan around football terms.

Game: The game simply represents our day in and day out responsibilities that demand our attention outside of child rearing. Basically everyday is a new game.
Signals: We affectionately called our regular connecting and conversational times throughout the day signals. These were our times before school, breakfast, lunches, dinner and so on. Staying connected in this way helped us understand how each player was doing in the overall game.
Huddle: A huddle gives our children freedom to request our time, they can interrupt us when they need to and let us know that they would like some of our time. Calling for a huddle simply lets us know that they have something they would like to talk about but it isn't urgent so we could talk at our next earliest convenience. We committed to finishing what we were currently working on, and then we would give them the time they need.
Time Out: The time out is the biggest. Our children were given permission to call a time out when they needed to talk with us. Calling a time out communicates in no uncertain terms, "I need you now." So the game would be stopped and complete undivided attention would be given to our child.

Working together to create this plan was a great experience in itself. Our children felt that we truly wanted to be there for them and it was evident through our willingness to talk openly about it and devise this plan. I believe it gave them a great sense of security, just knowing that we would drop everything if they needed us to.

Throughout their childhood and adolescence the time out was only called a few times, and we honored their request by making ourselves available to them. This brought a greater sense of security while affirming our love and commitment to them, and you know what? My boss even understood in those rare occasions when our children absolutely needed us. What difference did all of this make? We may never really know the full extent of this, but I will say, once in a while our adult child will still call home and affectionately say, 'I call a huddle.'

What value do we communicate to our children when we make ourselves available to them in this way? I believe it communicates that our children matter, we are deeply concerned for their wellbeing and our relationship together is of great importance. That goes a long way in supporting a healthy relationship and providing the sense of security our children need today.

Reflection

- In what ways have I shown that I am available to my child?
- How could I give my child the assurance that I am here when they need me no matter what?

Relevancy

Meeting our children at their greatest point of interest is a sure fire way to ensure we are relevant and increase the potential of a relational connection with them. As important as it is to intentionally create family rhythms that support relationship, and be available when they need us, it is equally important that these times be relevant to our children. If not, instead of creating an environment where connection will be natural, we will create an environment that our children will dread, try to avoid, or feel they must tolerate to maintain our approval. It's not just a matter of spending time together on a consistent basis; it's how we spend time together that makes the difference.

"It's not just a matter of spending time together on a consistent basis; it's how we spend time together that makes the difference."

For instance, I enjoy fishing and could spend hours out on the lake enjoying the sights, sounds and activity. Although my son would enjoy this, I know my daughter has other interests and would rather not sit in the boat for hours, even if I am good company. If I were to spend a couple of hours with her walking through the mall, it would be more relevant to her.

Relevancy speaks of our willingness to set aside our own personal preferences and engage in activity or conversation that is of interest to our children. It also means that we are willing to adapt as our children mature and change; what they enjoyed at 5 or 6 may be incredibly different than what they enjoy at 15 or 16. Do something they enjoy, and in most cases they will open up and talk with you if they know you truly want to listen.

> "We have taught the principle of 'in honor giving preference to one another' by having our children alternately pick activities or topics of conversation. In this way each one has the privilege of choosing and participating in something they really enjoy, but also gives them opportunity to honor others by participating in something they may not necessarily have chosen."
>
> Lynn

Reflection

- How much of our time together is spent focussing on my own interests and desires compared to the interests and desires of my children?
- If I had to change one thing that would make me more relevant to my child, what would it be?
- What am I willing to do in order to connect with my child in a relevant manner?

Exercise

Take some time and consider the following in relation to each of your children.

What is my child passionate about?

- What do they talk about the most?
- What keeps coming to the surface of conversations?
- What pre-occupies their minds?

What temperament/personality has God given my child, and how does this affect:
- How they interact with others?
- Their learning styles?
- How they interact within the family unit?
- Their friendships?
- Their schooling?
- Their social interactions?

What have I recognized God doing within their lives?
- What does He seem to be working on/developing within them as individuals?
- How can I practically encourage growth and maturity in these areas?

What strengths and/or abilities does my child have?
- Identify their strengths.
- Take time to affirm these.
- How can you begin encouraging your child in these areas?
- In what ways can you begin releasing more responsibility to them that compliments their growing ability?

Helpful Hint

Become a student of your child, watch, observe and pay attention to their interests and desires. Intentionally tailoring an activity or conversation that is relevant to them will increase their appreciation and respect for you, especially if they recognize that there is sacrifice on your part in doing so.

If you are having difficulty understanding the interests and desires of your child, ask them, and listen to their responses. Our children are the best source of information we have about themselves.

Transparency

As parents we have sometimes assumed that we must look like we have it 'all together' and if we let our children see our shortcomings and failures, they will lose respect for us. This couldn't be further from the truth; in fact, the opposite is true. Being vulnerable by admitting that we don't have it 'all together' and sharing our shortcomings and failures with our children actually increases their respect for us and brings humanness into our relationship that they can relate to. Think about this for a moment: our children cannot understand who we are becoming if they don't know who we were.

Listen as Suzanne shares what impact her mother's *transparency* has had upon her.

> "I respect my mother more because she has been honest with me about her life and the mistakes that she has made. At first I think she was hesitant to tell me about her teen years because of how bad she was, but it gave me a better understanding of just who my mom is and what she had to go through. Seeing what she dealt with and went through helped me know that she is someone I can go to if I need help in those areas and I am thankful she was honest and didn't hide her life from me."
>
> Suzanne, 15

Transparency builds trust, promotes authenticity, and openness within our relationships, whereas secrecy builds suspicion, promotes hypocrisy, and a relationship that is closed. One of the things our children cannot stand is hypocrisy within our lives, and making ourselves vulnerable through *transparency* helps prevent this.

"Transparency builds trust, promotes authenticity and openness within our relationships, whereas secrecy builds suspicion, promotes hypocrisy, and a relationship that is closed."

Realize we make ourselves vulnerable by being transparent with our children as a gift to them, not to fill our own needs. It's not about us, but about offering them a gift and in doing so we do not need to air all of our 'dirty laundry' out on the line for them to see. *Transparency* shares what is necessary in the moment so our children will know and understand that we, too, are human, have made mistakes and do not have it all together. Be sensitive to the maturity of your child; the *transparency* one needs from their parents in childhood is different than the *transparency* they need throughout adolescence.

If we desire an open, transparent and authentic relationship with our child, then we must initiate it by modeling *transparency* ourselves, honoring it as a value within our home and personal lives. When we fully accept our own humanness by admitting our faults, mistakes, and shortcomings we create an environment of trust, openness, and relatability in which it is safe for our children to do the same.

Making these four principles, *Consistency, Availability, Relevancy and Transparency,* a regular part of our lives will help in creating an environment in which relational connection is not only natural, but normal. We will begin finding that more often than not, our child is *opening* up, and giving us permission to touch the deeper areas of their lives, because they know they have a safe relational environment in which to do so.

Chapter 8

Asking

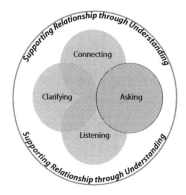

"When my parents started asking me questions and involving me in decision making I felt like I mattered to them. My opinion counted for something and I was no longer just a little kid who was expected to be seen and not heard."

Alex, 16

Asking is a powerful discipline for the Pro-Active Parent Coach. The very act of *asking* a question sets our children's mind toward finding an answer and creates space for additional information to emerge. This process leads us to a true understanding of what they are thinking, feeling and experiencing. The purpose for *asking* questions is multi-faceted:

- It honors and respects our child's uniqueness.
- It supports the development of an open and honest relationship.
- It engages our child's heart for greater discovery.
- It builds greater awareness within our children.
- It cooperates with our child's *Natural Growth Patterns*.
- It promotes responsibility within our children.
- It allows them to enter into meaningful conversation with us.

Communication is always taking place within our homes but the bigger question remains, "Is conversation taking place?" One dad in exasperation asked his son, "Dave, why don't you ever open up to me?" Imagine the dad's surprise when his son responded, "Well, Dad, you just don't ask the right questions." With a little discipline, and practice, *asking effective questions* is something every parent can do!

Our focus here, will be upon learning to ask effective questions that will help our children open up and talk.

Following are two examples, the first of closed communication and the second of open conversation. Notice the questions the parent asks and what makes them effective or ineffective at inviting the child into conversation.

Closed Communication	Open Conversation
"How was school today?" "Fine." *"What did you do?"* "Nothing." *"You must have done something, you spent 6 hours there!"* "No, not really. Can I go now Dad?" *"Where are you going?"* "Out." *"Out where?"* "I don't know, just out." *"When will you be home?"* "Later!" *"No matter how hard I try, you never let me through those walls you have built up around yourself. Go, and I hope you enjoy yourself, too!"*	*"Hey, Tony, how is it going today?"* "Don't ask!" *"That doesn't sound like the Tony I know, what's going on?"* "Don't worry about it. It is no big deal." *"Are you sure? It sounds to me like it might be. Maybe just talking about it will help you out a bit. No pressure, but if you would like to share, I'm here."* "Yeah, well, it might help." *"I'm all ears."* "Well, you know Gail, the girl I talked about a couple of weeks ago who was my Science lab partner?" *"Yes."* "I saw her talking with Mike outside the cafeteria today. They were laughing and joking, looking like they were having a great old time." *"Ohh?"*

"Yeah, it made me sick to my stomach and I couldn't concentrate the rest of the day."

"What were you thinking about?"

"Well, I couldn't get the two of them out of my head. I mean, I thought she liked me. We had a great time together doing the Science lab, and well, I thought we had some sort of connection and I really like her. She's fun, witty and smart. She even gave me her phone number and we've been chatting almost every night after supper. Then this today; I don't know what to think anymore."

Reflection

- What attitude differences did you see between the parents throughout both conversations?
- What difference did you notice about the questions asked in both conversations?
- Which group of questions best represents what you currently ask your children, questions that close communication or questions that open conversation?

Examining the two conversations above, we notice the first dad used closed questions when attempting to start a conversation with his son. Additionally, when the conversation didn't go as he expected, he resorted to using sarcasm which further pushes his child away. Closed questions are not effective at inviting someone into deeper conversation.

In the second conversation we see an entirely different environment. First the dad recognizes something 'out of character' with his son's response and asks about it. This speaks of the relationship that they already share. Secondly, he doesn't force himself upon the son but makes himself available if the son wants to pursue conversation. Thirdly, after his son agrees, Dad asks open questions and authentically listens while empathizing with him. Doing this allowed the son to answer freely, leading to a more casual but richer heartfelt conversation that helped Dad understand what was really taking place.

"Communication is always taking place within our homes, but the bigger question remains, 'Is conversation taking place?'"

There is no doubt that questions are powerful. They can enrich relationship, drawing our children out in conversation, and promote a healthy interdependence. On the other hand, ineffective questions act as a barrier, preventing depth of conversation, shut our children down and can promote independent thinking.

Transitioning from *telling* to *asking* within our parenting creates an environment that supports relationship by;

- Encouraging our children to open up.
- Valuing their contribution.
- Encouraging their progress with decision making.
- Honoring them for who they are.
- Communicating respect.
- Stating in an unmistakable way, "I believe in you."

Contrast that with the message we communicate to our children when we maintain a posture of telling. When I tell instead of ask I communicate;

- You are to be seen, not heard.
- Your contribution is not valued.
- You are not capable of making decisions.
- You cannot handle life without my help.
- Performance is more important than relationship.
- Says in an unmistakable way, "You're not good enough."

Effective questions lead us on an incredible journey into the heart and minds of our children where the landscape is marked by wonder, excitement, and discovery. It breathes new life into our relationship as we grow in our understanding of who our children truly are and what they are becoming. As we continue coaching in this way, we will realize that our children and teens are much more capable of carrying on intelligent conversation than we have often given them credit for. The depth of conversation we can have and the growth we experience within our relationship together make *asking effective questions* worth the effort.

What Kids are Saying

How do you feel when you are consistently told what to do?

"It makes me feel like a little child, like I can't do anything right."
Robyn, 14

"I get the feeling that I am not trusted, and they feel they must keep a close eye on my every move."
Eric, 16

"It's like I don't know anything and can't figure things out for myself."
Alan, 14

"I feel as if my parents never listen to me or really care to understand me. It's more like this: 'Do what I say and you will be fine, don't do what I say and your life will be a mess.'"
Roberta, 16

"To me it's like I don't really matter. I sometimes wonder if my parents are more concerned about how they look to others than what I am experiencing and feeling inside."
Sarah-Jane, 15

What Makes a Question Effective?

The enriched relationship and additional value of *asking effective questions* is highly motivating. So much so, we might be tempted to run right over to little Johnny or Jenny and ask some questions right now, expecting that as we do, they will open their little hearts right up to us.

This may, or more likely, will not be our experience. Remember, children open up as a result of relational closeness, and relational closeness is only developed over time. One of our goals in *asking effective questions* is to cultivate a healthy and supportive relationship. It gives our children an opportunity to share and grow in their trust for us. When they know we genuinely want to listen and will do so without passing judgment, they will open up. As with any new practice, it will take time, effort and consistency before our children adapt to this new approach and open up. Take heart and be encouraged, as we hone and practice these skills, our children will see that we are sincere and will begin to respond.

Characteristics of Effective Questions

Effective Questions Support Relationship by:

- Fostering a healthy relational environment.
- Inviting our children into conversation.
- Encouraging deeper thought.
- Assisting in giving clarity, understanding and perspective.
- Focusing on learning and discovery.
- Challenging current thinking.
- Helping children evaluate themselves and their experiences.
- Considering a different perspective.
- Looking at issues from a different point of view.
- Raising awareness and understanding.
- Promoting responsibility.
- *Exploring Possibilities*, facts, thoughts and feelings.
- *Assessing Desire.*
- *Securing Commitment.*
- *Encouraging Progress.*

Much More Than a '?' Mark

Transitioning from *telling* to *asking effective questions* involves much more than simply tagging a '?' mark onto the end of our sentences. How we ask is as important as what we ask and this requires intentionality on our part. To ask effective questions, first consider the *characteristics of effective questions*, and then carefully craft the questions you will ask. At first this may seem like hard work, but be encouraged; over time, *asking effective questions* will become quite normal and natural within conversation. Soon you will discover you are *asking effective questions* without really thinking about it.

Observe the following conversation between a parent and their teen who just returned from camp. Ask yourself: "Do the questions asked by the parent here, have the characteristics of effective questions?"

Conversation

"Did you enjoy camp this year?"
"Yes."
"Did you connect with your counselors? I mean, how did you get along with them? Were they nice?"
"Umm, I don't know, well I guess so."

"Did you make lots of new friends or just a few?"
"Just a few."
"What was your favorite part of camp this year, the games?"
"No, it was the worship."

Reflection

- Were these questions effective at getting the child to open up? Why or why not?
- How would you describe this conversation?
- Who did most of the thinking and talking within this conversation?

Let's take a closer look at the questions asked above.

1. *"Did you enjoy camp this year?"* This is a closed question, which can be answered with a simple yes or no. Very little thought is needed on the child's part and doesn't invite further conversation.

2. *"Did you connect with your counselors? I mean how did you get along with them? Were they nice?"* A barrage of questions can take place when the parent has asked a question using phrases or terminology their child may not understand. In an attempt to clarify what 'connect' means, another question is asked, but once again this creates a closed question. Too many questions at once make it difficult for our children to answer thoughtfully. Additionally, it may give them an opportunity to simply answer one question and ignore the others.

3. *"Did you make lots of new friends or just a few?"* Once again this is a closed question in that it only offers a choice between two responses; 'lots' or 'a few'.

4. *"What was your favorite part of camp this year, the games?"* This begins as a potentially effective question which could encourage more conversation if the presumption of games was left off. For instance, the child may say what their favorite part of camp was, which could be followed up by asking, "What made that your favorite?" By putting an answer in our child's mouth we communicate, 'I already know you and there isn't much more you can tell me.' This shuts our children down because they feel we don't truly want to know them or we simply 'know it all anyway, so why bother?'

"Transitioning from telling to asking effective questions involves much more than simply tagging a '?' mark onto the end of our sentences."

With all of the questions above we see that the child is passive while the parent is doing most of the talking and thinking. When we ask effective questions, the opposite is true. We ask, and then give our child the time they need to think through and respond thoughtfully to our questions. By doing this, we create the space necessary for open conversation. It allows more information to come out so that we can truly understand what our child is thinking, feeling and experiencing.

When we experience a conversation similar to what we observed above, we tend to believe our children do not want to open up and talk with us. This couldn't be further from the truth. In fact, they do desire to open up; we simply need to create an environment that encourages them to do so.

Take a moment and observe the same scenario as above but notice how effective questions draw the child into a more meaningful conversation.

Coaching Conversation

"Tell me about camp this year."

"Camp was great this year, I love Braeside camp."

"That sounds incredible! What do you love about it?"

"Well, lots of things. I get to go away for a week with friends and during this time I also get to see old friends that I made at camp in years past. Some I only get to see at camp once a year. I know Facebook® keeps us in touch, but I like getting to see them and spend time with them in person."

"Sounds amazing."

"Yeah it is."

"Is there anything else that you love about it?"

"The counselors are great too. They make camp so fun."

"In what way?"

"Well, they get along so well with us students, you just know that they care about us and they treat us like people, not little kids. They're also in charge of the games and they always choose games that have a purpose, and coordinate in some way with the lessons we're learning. Oh, and the teacher this year was really cool. He did cartooning while he taught and some of the kids got to take the pictures home as gifts."

"What kind of things did they teach?"

"This year the focus was on 'Our value as individuals.' We were challenged not to let anyone despise us because of our age, but to live in a way that people would see us and glorify God."

"Sounds like a great focus for teen camp. What was it that made the biggest difference in your life this week?"

"Well, the speaker talked about how each person, no matter how old they are, has a purpose in life. He challenged us with stories from the Bible about Joseph, David and Timothy. Although they were young, God accepted and worked through them in powerful ways to bring about change in His kingdom. I think what hit me the most was the fact that even at 13 years of age I have a purpose and God wants me to discover it."

Reflection

- Were these questions effective at getting the child to open up? Why or why not?
- How would you describe this conversation?
- Who did most of the thinking and talking within this conversation?

Let's take a closer look at the questions used in this conversation.

1. *"Tell me about camp this year."* This is an open invitation for the child to share whatever is on their mind. It is non-directing and very open, giving the child freedom to take the conversation where they want to by sharing what is most important to them.

2. *"That sounds incredible! What do you love about it?"* The parent focuses in on a key word the child used, 'love', and asks them to elaborate about what they love about camp.

3. *"Sounds amazing."* This is an affirmation of the child's experience but also lets the child know the parent is listening and engaged in the conversation.

4. *"Is there anything else that you love about it?"* Asking for 'anything else' allows them to continue thinking about what they love about camp. Draws them into further reflection and sharing which may bring out some great insights, learning, or lead to further supporting their growth through coaching.

5. *"In what way?"* Allows the child to explore what they appreciated about the counselors without leading their thoughts in any way. This again allows the child to share openly and brings more information into the conversation to give the parent a greater understanding of what is taking place within the child's mind.

6. *"What kind of things did they teach?"* This question allows the child to revisit the topics that were taught at camp. This brings more information into the conversation and allows the child to reflect upon their experience in more detail. It could potentially lead to a coaching conversation that would support their growth in areas that were taught at camp.

7. *"Sounds like a great focus for teen camp. What was it that made the biggest difference in your life this week?"* The parent here takes a moment to affirm the value of what was taught at camp and then pushes their child to reflect more about what difference this has made in their life. This is a great opportunity to foster the child's growth by having them reflect and apply what they have learned at camp. In this way, we leverage learning through coaching making it truly transformational.

This conversation illustrates how well effective questions invite conversation and open the door for exploration. The child in this account did most of the thinking and talking as the parent simply asked effective questions and authentically listened.

Coaching conversations, as you will discover, have a unique way of opening a child's heart and providing parents with opportunities to support their child's growth in many areas. In the preceding conversation we can see a coaching opportunity opening up in relation to the child's life purpose. Keying in on what the child said, "I think what hit me the most was the fact that even at 13 years of age I have a purpose and God wants me to discover it," would allow us to naturally transition to *Supporting* their *Growth* through further coaching.

Reflection

In light of this coaching opportunity, take a few moments and think about what question(s) you could ask your child if they said, "I think what hit me the most was the fact that even at 13 years of age I have a purpose and God wants me to discover it." Write your question(s) here.

Effective Questions are Almost Always Open Questions

Questions that invite relational conversation, capture the child's heart, and assist us in gaining understanding, are almost always open ended questions. They invite conversation, beg for deeper thought and catalyze relational closeness. Closed questions, on the other hand, do not stimulate conversation or deeper thinking because they can be answered simply with a 'yes,' 'no,' or nod of the head.

Open questions, therefore, are a key component of a healthy parent coaching conversation and typically begin with 'What,' 'How,' 'Where,' 'Who,' 'When' or statements such as 'tell me more about...' or 'help me understand ...'.

> **"The purposes of a man's heart are deep waters, but a man of understanding draws them out."**
> Proverbs 20:5 (NIV)

Helpful Hint

If you find that you are prone to asking leading questions, and you catch yourself mid-sentence, you can open the question by adding something as simple as, "or something else." For example, "What was your favorite thing about camp, the games, or was it something else?"

Exercise

In a practical way, how could you convert a typical parenting question like, "How was school today?" into an effective question that might invite deeper conversation.

Take some time and create '5' open ended 'what,' questions that you could potentially ask your child this week which would encourage them to open up. In this way, you will be better prepared to engage your child in conversation and hone your newfound skill at the next opportunity.

• "Tell me about what happened at school today."

• "What was one significant thing that happened today at school?"

•

•

•

Transitioning from Telling to Asking

A common pitfall new parent coaches fall into is disguising their advice and/or opinions by placing a '?' mark at the end of their sentence. In doing so they feel they are effectively asking questions instead of simply telling their children what to do, but are they? Let's take a closer look at the following common parenting questions and see what is really taking place.

Common Parenting Questions

- "Should you do the dishes before going outside to play?"
- "Don't you think you're a bit too young for that?"
- "Could you do your homework first and then spend some time with your friends?"
- "Wouldn't it be better to get your education, before worrying about a job?"
- "You don't want to do that, do you?"
- "Would it help if you began your day with devotions?"
- "Would it help to pray about that before you make a decision?"

Did you recognize it? Although these were asked as questions, they are not questions at all. Rather, they are statements telling our children what to do with a '?' mark tagged on the end. Let's look at these again, but this time with a few words struck out, which reveals the 'questions' real intent; to tell instead of ask.

- "~~Should you~~ do the dishes before going outside to play?"
- "~~Don't you think~~ you're a bit too young for that?"
- "~~Could you~~ do your homework first and then spend some time with your friends?"
- "~~Wouldn't it be better to~~ get your education before worrying about a job?"
- "You don't want to do that, ~~do you~~?"
- "~~Would it help if you~~ begin your day with devotions?"
- "~~Would it help to~~ pray about that before you make a decision?"

Is this revealing for you? If so, don't be discouraged or overwhelmed. This is common, especially in the beginning, but the fact that you recognize it is a step in the right direction toward *asking effective questions*. With practice you will soon discover that it is not only easy but enjoyable because of the depth of conversation it encourages.

Exercise

Take a few moments and convert the following statements into effective questions.

Questions that 'Tell.'	Open Questions
"You don't want to do that, do you?"	"Tell me more about this; what attracts you to it?"
"Would it help if you began your day with devotions?"	
"Would it help to pray about that before you make a decision?"	
"Don't you think you're a bit too young for that?"	

Helpful Hint

If you discover that you are prone to asking closed questions, try putting a 'what' or 'how' at the front of your questions. This will often turn a closed question into an open one.

Closed Question	Observation
"Do you think that is a good decision?"	This can be simply answered, 'Yes,' or 'No.' If the answer is 'Yes,' it begs a follow up from the parent of 'Why?' Asking why unintentionally sets our children on the defensive. They will often feel they have to justify or defend themselves and this often shuts a conversation down.
Neutral Open Question	**Observation**
"How do you think this decision will affect you?"	By putting 'how' at the beginning of this question it becomes more neutral and open. It causes our children to reflect more and doesn't leave our children with the feeling that they must justify or defend themselves. Instead, it sets their mind upon more reflection, considering the potential consequences the decision might bring.

Resisting our old patterns of *telling* by *asking* open questions supports relationship and conversation at a much deeper level. It is an incredible way to communicate that we value and appreciate who they are becoming and invites them into deeper, richer relationship with us.

> **"Our children desire to open up, we simply need to create an environment that encourages them to do so."**

If our children are accustomed to us simply telling them what to do, transitioning to the *asking* model will seem a little awkward for them in the beginning. They may be hesitant to open up, and need reassurance from you to do so. Don't be discouraged! When they recognize that you genuinely want their input, are listening for their response, and can be trusted, they will warm up to the idea and open up to you. Be patient though, at first you may have to prove yourself to them.

Although the *Supporting Relationship through Understanding* Model utilizes open and indirect questions to gain understanding, as we move into the second stage of our model, *Supporting Growth* you will notice that we employ direct questions as we *Assess Desire*, *Secure Commitment* and *Encourage Progress*. In the mean time, let's begin *asking effective questions* and simply enjoy the rich relationship that we can have with our children.

Supplement: Going Deeper with Questions

Be Careful Using 'Why' Questions

Did you notice that 'Why' was not included when creating effective questions? The reason for this is; we must exercise extreme caution when asking the 'Why' question. Although 'Why' questions are sometimes appropriate in conversation, by asking our children 'Why?' they often feel their motives are being called into question and this puts them on the defensive where they feel they must justify themselves.

Observe how 'Why' questions can affect our children and their openness in conversation.

Positive Use of 'Why?'

A. The parent has already been engaged in conversation with their child about why they looked upset when they arrived home from school. Throughout conversation it is brought out that Johnny has been bullying some of the other kids at school and the parent here wants to turn their child's attention, in an empathetic way, toward the reason Johnny may be bullying others.

Conversation	Observation
"I'm glad you opened up; I didn't know this was taking place at all. It helps me understand why you were so upset. Can we talk about Johnny a little bit?" "Yeah, sure." "When you think about Johnny, why do you think he might be acting like this?" "I don't know, he's a real jerk." "Well, he might be acting like one, but I think there must be something more to it. What might that be?" "I don't know everything for sure, but I guess there are probably reasons why he is acting like this. I heard that his Mom just left home about a month ago because his Dad was running around with someone else. I guess this new woman has moved in with them and he doesn't get along that well with her.	Wanting the child to develop empathy, this parent turns the child's attention to the bully by asking a 'why' question which causes the child to consider other factors in the bully's life that may be affecting him. The use of why in this scenario is non-threatening and opens the conversation up because the focus is upon another child.

Why can be appropriate in conversation when we use it carefully to broaden our children's perspective in a non-threatening way. More often than not, though, 'why' is used and perceived in a negative way. Consider the following questions and how they might affect our children if we ask them.

- "Why are you always doing that?"
- "Why can't you be more like your sister/brother?"
- "Why can't you_____?"

- "Why must you always _____?"
- "Why don't you become more involved in _____?"

These 'Why' questions carry with them a sense that we are questioning our children's character, actions, or decisions, naturally putting them on the defensive. When our children feel as though they must defend themselves, depending on their personality, they will either grow more aggressive and 'fight' or they will withdraw and simply shut down. Either response is detrimental to *Supporting Relationship* .

> **"More often than not, 'why' is used and perceived in a negative way."**

Negative Use of 'Why?'

B. The parent in the following example is getting a little stressed over preparing dinner for company who will be arriving in a short time. Mom has been preparing to ensure everything is just right for their company. Although the entire family is aware that company is coming and has said they would help with preparations, Alan, their teen aged son, comes home from school and plops down in front of the television. Mom approaches him to request his help preparing for company to arrive.

Conversation	Observation
"Alan, honey, I don't think you have time to watch television right now. I could really use your help out here." "I'm tired, Mom. Just give me a few minutes to relax." "No, honey, not today. The Smith's will be here in just over an hour and I want this house cleaned up." "The Smith's? They know who we are, we don't need to clean up the house to impress them." "OK, enough is enough. Why do you always act like this?" "Act like what?" "You know very well we have company coming over. We've talked about it, planned on it, and here you are, coming home from school and just flopping down in front of the television like nothing is going on." "Well, maybe I don't think it's such a big deal what our house looks like. If they are friends they'll take us as we are; besides, aren't they coming to see us and not the house? So what difference does all that extra work really make? You worry yourself for nothing when no one really cares. . . ."	Asking 'Why do you always act like this?' puts Alan on the defensive and he turns it back on Mom by asking what she means. She has a choice here; stop and cool down, or describe what she is feeling right now and risk a relational conflict. We recognize that this escalates into a full scale argument which only serves to push Alan away.

Reflection

- What feeling did Mom's 'Why' question stir within you?
- What insight does that give you about the use of 'Why' questions?
- How could Mom have approached Alan differently in this situation which would have encouraged a different response from Alan?

Do you sense the difference? 'Why' questions often sound confrontational and put our child on the defensive, creating needless tension between us. The perception is that we are judging and criticizing them which puts them in a position where they feel they must justify, back pedal or defend themselves.

When asking 'Why' questions we should not be surprised if the mood within our conversation changes, and our child reverts to short, curt answers, or simply shuts down. Taking time to rephrase a 'Why' question may foster a more open and positive environment for conversation while encouraging them to be more reflective.

Exercise

Converting 'Why' questions to more neutral sounding questions will maintain a more relaxed and open conversational environment. Take a few moments now and practice converting 'Why' questions to more neutral questions. Use the space provided below.

Why Question	Open Neutral Question
"Why did you do that?"	"What led you to make that decision?"
"Why did you treat your friend like that?"	
"Why don't you just talk to your teacher about it?"	
"Why didn't you get your homework done?"	

Leading Questions

Leading questions have an implied answer within them. In other words, we are 'putting words in our child's mouth.' For example,

> "When are you going to speak to your teacher about that?"
> "Are you excited about that?"

In the first example the parent's expectation is stated within the question, 'You are going to speak to your teacher about that.' This fails to help our child *explore possibilities* and have a choice about which to pursue. In the second question, the child's feelings are presumed, which doesn't allow the child to articulate what he or she is truly feeling.

Exercise

Take a moment and convert the following leading questions into neutral questions which will allow the child to explore the possibilities for themselves.

Original Leading Question	Open Question
"When are you going to speak to your teacher about that?"	"What do you need to do now?"
"Are you excited about that?"	
"Would talking to Janet help smooth things over between you?"	
"Would it help if you prayed about it?"	

The Barrage of Questions

A barrage of questions is a string of questions tied together within one sentence, for example,

> "What happened, when did it happen, and how did you feel?"

This can be overwhelming and prevents our children from giving thoughtful consideration to each question. It can also be an opportunity for our children to select which question they want to answer and avoid the others.

When asking questions, intentionally ask one and allow sufficient time for thought, reflection and a meaningful response. Resist the temptation to fill silence too quickly.

Embrace Silence

Asking effective questions may be met with silence. Resist the temptation of jumping in too quickly with another comment or question and allow silence to promote deeper thought. Silence gives our child the opportunity to examine the question, consider it fully, and how they will respond to the question.

Additionally, if there is not an immediate response to a question and silence falls, it may indicate that our question has become powerful because they have not considered it before. When we allow silence, and patiently wait for our children to respond fully without interruption, we create an environment of deeper reflection, open, and heartfelt conversation. Breaking silence too quickly short circuits their thought process and robs them of the opportunity for greater reflection.

Consider, just for a moment, that the average person waits less than 5 seconds before they begin talking again. What internal work are we potentially short-circuiting by talking too soon? If we find we have a tendency to jump in too quickly, we could discipline ourselves by waiting twice as long before speaking again just to see what additional information comes out.

Practice
- If your child doesn't respond immediately to a question, resist the temptation to dive right back in. Instead wait an additional few seconds before rephrasing or clarifying that they understood your question.
- Develop the habit of pausing for an additional few seconds after your child has stopped speaking. This gives them more freedom to think about the question, their response, and see if other thoughts surface.
- Be aware of your own comfort level with silence. Does it make you uncomfortable? When silence falls do you have an urge to speak to break the silence? If so, discipline yourself to remain quiet for an extra few seconds and see what that silence draws out of your child.

Helpful Hint

Do you anticipate difficulty in transitioning from telling to *asking effective questions*? Here is a practical way to help you with that transition. Ask your child to partner with you in your growth and development in this area. Let them know that you are making a commitment to change because you want to understand them better and ask if you can enlist their help. Give them permission to stop you and tell you when you ask a closed question or a statement disguised as a question and every time they catch you doing so, you will give them $1.00. This could become a fun relational connection and also make you partners in your own growth. Not only that, they may be motivated by the prospect of gaining some extra spending money.

Remember: The purpose of asking effective questions is to 'draw out' our children so that we may truly understand what they are thinking, feeling, and experiencing. To truly understand though, we must move beyond asking effective questions to authentically listening, so, let's turn our attention now toward the discipline of listening.

Chapter 9

Listening

> "I remember the first time I felt like I was truly being listened to. It was shocking for me because I expected to be cut off and given a lecture, but I wasn't. They simply listened as I talked. It was like they truly wanted to know and understand who I really was and what made me tick. It made me happy and I felt like an adult not a little child. I found myself wanting to talk to this person more and more, especially when I was facing difficult times. I now have someone I can count on, knowing they will be there for me no matter what. That is why I never speak with my parents, because I never get that kind of response, and yet, they still wonder why I won't open up to them."
>
> Sarah, 15

If we are going to *ask effective questions*, it would make sense that we would listen in order to gain understanding. *Listening* connects with one of our children's greatest felt needs; to be known and understood. It gives greater clarity and helps us truly understand what our children are thinking, experiencing and feeling. The act of listening itself opens hearts for deeper, more meaningful conversation.

Consider for a moment the people we regularly interact with, those individuals in our lives who truly listen to understand. The environment they create for us through *listening* gives us a sense that we are;

      accepted,
          valued,
              respected,
                  appreciated, and
                      understood.

"If we are going to ask effective questions, it would make sense that we would listen in order to gain understanding."

In short, when someone truly listens to us, they are saying in an undeniable way, 'I love you.' When we feel loved we lower our defenses, let down our guard and open our hearts up for examination.

Contrast this with someone who doesn't listen. Do we sense the same love and care? Do we feel safe and lower our defenses? Will we openly share from the heart? Probably not!

Read through the following conversation and think about how this experience would affect you.

"Hey, how's it going?"

"Hi there, I'm glad I ran into you. Honestly, it's been a rough week, I . . ."

"Oh yeah, I know what you mean! Mine has been rough too."

"Well, no actually, it's not about me personally. See my Mom, she's . . ."

"You're Mom? You know I was thinking about her the other day, I saw her last week and thought, 'Man, she looks good for her age.' My Mom and Dad are in Florida right now enjoying life as snowbirds. I can't wait until I retire and I can follow in their footsteps, relax through the winters in a sunny place. Man, that's the life. If only I were rich enough to do that now! Thinking about retirement, what do you plan on doing when you retire?"

"Well, ahh, you know I haven't given it much thought this week."

"That's too bad, you know what they say, 'If you fail to plan, you plan to fail.' Well it's been really nice catching up with you, but I have to run, some pressing appointments to get to. Just remember, if there is anything I can help you with, I am always here for you!"

"Yeah, thanks . . . I'll keep that in mind."

Reflection

Thinking about this conversation, what affect would being listened to, or more accurately, not being listened to, in this way have upon you?

- When you sense that you are not being listened to, what is your gut reaction?
- How does that make you feel?
- Do you open up and share the deeper things in your life, or simply decide not to bother?

What kind of person do we tend to open up with?
What characteristics do they have?
What kind of environment do they create for us?

To help you with this, think of someone that you know who genuinely listens to you. When you're talking with them, you know that they are *connecting*, asking, *listening* and *clarifying* as needed to ensure they understand what you are saying. In other words, they are fully present with you, their minds are not wandering, they are not interrupting or changing the subject. They are fully engaged in listening.

In the box below describe how that makes you feel.

```
┌─────────────────────────────────────────────────────────┐
│                                                         │
│                                                         │
│                                                         │
│                                                         │
│                                                         │
│                                                         │
└─────────────────────────────────────────────────────────┘
```

Your description may include the following, I felt . . .

- Accepted.
- Valued.
- Respected.
- Appreciated.
- Cared for.
- Not judged.
- Safe.
- Understood.
- I had permission to explore my thoughts, ideas and dreams.
- I was free to be myself.

The list may continue to grow but there is one undeniable characteristic: in that environment, you feel *loved*. *Listening*, above all else, communicates our love for one another and opens the door to touching the deeper areas of our lives.

It would serve us well to remember that the environment we need and desire for ourselves, is the very environment our children need and desire for themselves. The environment that we need to lower our defenses, to open up and risk sharing the deeper matters of our heart, is the very environment our children need. As parents we are in the best position and have the greatest opportunity to create this environment.

> **"In short, when someone truly listens to us, they are saying in an undeniable way, 'I love you.'"**

To Listen is to Love

Our children, including teens, are more interested in opening up to us than we give them credit for. The majority we have encountered throughout our ministry have affirmed they would welcome this kind of relationship with their parents, but have felt they could not openly share without fear of being judged, rejected or preached at.

> "I'd love it if I could sit down and have a heart to heart with my parents. But if they knew what I was thinking at times, they'd go ballistic. It's much easier on all of us to just keep things a secret."
>
> Sonja, 16

That's a tough statement to swallow but for many it is their reality. What is it that often keeps us from authentically listening and understanding our child? In two short words, *self control*.

In coaching terms this is called *Self Management*. In spiritual terms it is an evidence of the work of the Spirit within our lives; *Self Control* (Galatians 5:22). It is our ability as parents to set aside our

> personal opinions,
> > agendas,
> > > preferences,
> > > > pride,
> > > > > defensiveness,
> > > > > > judgments, and
> > > > > > > appearances,

in order to fully understand and maintain a connection with our child. *Self Management/ Control* helps us to stay connected with our child so that we can listen to understand, as opposed to

> jumping to conclusions,
> > talking over,
> > > interrupting or
> > > > lecturing our children.

These simply serve to push our children away and close them down.

Authentically *listening*, in this way, communicates unconditional love, creating an environment of trust and openness in conversation which supports relationship together. If we jump to conclusions, make judgments or begin lecturing our children they will simply shut down, feeling as though they cannot be honest with us and they, like Sonja, will feel it is 'much easier on all of us to just keep things a secret.'

Managing our own emotions will keep our minds clear and focused, allowing us the freedom to give our children the full and undivided attention they deserve. Observe the effect *listening* in this way had upon the following two teens.

"When I experienced my Dad genuinely listening to me, it was the most amazing feeling I ever had. It was a closeness that I'd never felt before. I felt respected and most importantly, I felt loved. I felt like me and my Dad could communicate without fear, without feeling judged or having his opinion thrown in my face. My thought exactly was, 'Wow, he actually cares!' If I were to say how I felt in one word, it would be, loved! There is no other word for it."

Patricia, 16

"Unlike some of my friend's parents, mine take time to listen to me. The sense I get is that they really want to understand and know me as a person, rather than simply 'fix me.' I think they are really trying to help me learn from my mistakes and make better decisions. I appreciate the fact that my parents respect me in this way."

Benjamin, 17

From our children's perspective, even as teens, *listening* without passing judgment or trying to 'fix them,' communicates "I love you!" Or "I respect you," loud and clear.

Moving Beyond Skill to the Heart of Listening

Active *listening* skills like eye contact, body posture, the occasional 'uh huh,' 'yes,' or 'OK' which acknowledge that we are listening are important and can help us stay focused, but they are no substitute for authentically listening. Let me illustrate in this way.

> **"He who restrains his words has knowledge, And he who has a cool spirit is a man of understanding."**
> Proverbs 17:27
> (NASB)

When I am in conversation with my child,

- I can put aside what I am currently doing to look interested.
- I can avoid looking around the room, at the computer screen or television.
- I can make eye contact to appear as though I am focused upon them.
- I can work at keeping an open body posture to conceal any discomfort with what they are saying.
- I can even nod and make 'verbal' noises which indicate I am paying attention.

However, at the same time

- I can be entertaining my concerns about an upcoming work deadline.
- I can be mulling over thoughts for a presentation I need to make.
- I can be rehearsing a conversation with my 'ex' over visitation rights.
- I can be planning our evening meal.
- I can be wondering how long this will take before I get back to more important things.
- Ultimately, I can be thinking about anything other than what my child is saying at the moment.

Technique alone is not enough. It makes us appear as though;

> We care, when in fact we don't;
> We're interested, when in fact we're not;
> We're listening, when in reality we are not listening at all.

On the other hand, authentic listening flows naturally from the value we place upon our relationship.

> I listen, because I value what you have to say;
> I listen, because I want to understand;
> I listen, because I love you.

Skills and technique simply serve as tools that help us give our children what is already within our heart more effectively. Without heart, skill and technique alone will seem hollow, superficial and may even be perceived as manipulation by our children. If we truly value relationship with them, effective questions and excellent *listening* technique will make that value shine through in our conversations together.

The Moment Truth Catalyzed a Change

"Daddy." "Daddy." Her voice was soft, distant and hollow at first. "Daddy"! she continued a little louder but not yet clear. "Pastor Greg! Are you listening to me?" These words shook me from the prison of my thoughts as I recognized my daughter had been speaking for some time and I missed everything she said. "Daddy, I thought you were listening to me. What were you thinking about?"

Although sitting in a familiar place, sharing time together as we often do, my mind was elsewhere. I was involved in another conversation, one that started much earlier in the day and as a result, I missed most of what my little girl was saying. A sick feeling stirred in the pit of my stomach as I looked into her inquisitive eyes and confessed, "I'm sorry, honey, I am very distracted today. I'll try to do better, what was it you were saying again?"

This experience taught me two valuable lessons; first, the outward impression we give may not accurately represent what is taking place inside of us. Secondly, I cannot multitask with words! In that moment, I renewed my commitment to be fully present when engaged in conversation.

Taking our Thoughts Captive

The difference between a great listener and a poor listener is found within their ability to manage one critical component - the mind. Multitasking with words is the fundamental challenge to *listening* well because it is very difficult for our brains to do two things with words at the same time.

> **"The heart of the discerning acquires knowledge, for the ears of the wise seek it out."**
> Proverbs 18:15 (NIV)

Our child is speaking (that's one thing involving words) and at the same time we have a second, unseen conversation taking place within our mind (which makes two things). Because our brain cannot process both conversations at the same time we miss bits and pieces of the conversation as we switch between the audible and the conversation within our heads.

If we have missed parts of the conversation, how can we truly understand what is being spoken? To listen well, we must turn off the conversation within our mind and give our full undivided attention to what our child is saying.

Tuning out our own thoughts and tuning into our child's thoughts is essential to *listening* but can be a difficult discipline at the best of times. When we realize that we've tuned out in conversation we should immediately acknowledge it and ask our children to back up and restate what they were saying.

This can be accomplished very easily by saying something like,
- "I'm sorry, I missed your last comment, could you repeat that for me?"
- "Would you repeat that for me again? I tuned out for a moment."
- "I'm really interested in what you're saying, but was distracted for a moment. Could you go back and repeat that for me?"

It's important that we don't worry about our image at this time. 'What will they think if they know I wasn't paying attention?' Realize first, they probably already know, and secondly, it brings credibility back into the relationship when we admit our shortcomings but affirm that we want to understand and not let distractions keep us from doing so.

Exercise

Sit down with one of your children and let them know you want to honor and respect them by becoming a better listener. Ask them if they are willing to help you out, which may become a fun exercise giving you an opportunity for relational connection. Invite them to share anything they would like with you; it's their choice what topic to talk about. You, on the other hand, make a commitment to listen and ask open questions as necessary to gain an understanding of what they are saying.

Try this for 10-15 minutes and immediately afterward ask yourself the following questions.
- How difficult was it to stay focused on what my child was saying?
- What other things did I think about during the conversation?
- What prompted or stirred those thoughts within my mind?
- How often did I 'problem solve', compose my response or next question while my child was speaking?
- Did I become concerned about whether or not it 'looked like' I was listening?
- What does this tell me about my listening ability?

Changing Perspective

Sometimes we're guilty of only *listening* long enough to hear what we expect or want to hear. Then we quickly jump in with our own thoughts and ideas, thinking we have understood. This leaves our children feeling frustrated, disrespected and sometimes feeling as though parents don't really care to understand them.

"When I ask you to listen to me and you start giving advice, you have not done what I asked. When I ask you to listen to me and you feel you have to do something to solve my problems, you have failed me, as strange as that may seem. And if you want to talk, wait a few moments for your turn and I promise I'll listen to you."

Anonymous

Take a moment and think about the reason we *listen* to our children. What is the purpose of *listening*? Do we listen so we can diagnose their problems and offer solutions? If this is our belief, we will break the healthy communication cycle and without realizing it, subtly push our children toward someone else who will offer them an unbiased listening ear.

Or,

Do we listen to engage the heart, support relationship, gain understanding and create a safe environment for our children to open up in? If our primary focus is relationship, our children will learn they can trust opening up to us and will give us permission to coach the deeper matters of their heart.

Common Internal Distractions

- Analyzing our child's 'problem.'
- Trying to guess where the conversation is headed.
- Formulating the next great question we will ask.
- Discomfort with the topic of conversation.
- Composing our response before they finish speaking.
- Thinking: 'I know what your issue is!'
- Entering into a mental argument with our child while they are talking.
- Rehearsing our responses.
- Formulating judgments.
- Focusing on maintaining an open posture when we notice we are becoming defensive.
- Strongly disagreeing with something our child has said or done, and allowing our mind to focus on that.
- Lack of interest in the topic of conversation.
- Feeling as though this is an interruption.
- Interrupting and expressing our thoughts or opinions.
- Wondering if we look like we're paying attention.
- Something piques our curiosity and in thinking about this we miss what they are saying.

Leveraging Curiosity to our Advantage

The most effective parent coaches seem to have a natural curiosity about them. Using curiosity to their advantage, they draw their children out in meaningful conversation. Curiosity is a unique characteristic. It can either set our minds wandering, or become a guide to greater understanding.

The following is how curiosity works negatively within conversation.

1. Within every conversation a common obstacle emerges.
2. We become curious about a word, a statement or body language.
3. We begin trying to identify their problem.
4. We look for indicators to confirm our diagnosis.
5. We develop a potential solution to their problem.
6. We develop a strategy to get them to see and embrace our solution.
7. We look for an opportunity to break into the conversation.
8. We tell our child what we see and try to convince them to embrace our solution or way of thinking.

> **Whoever is patient has great understanding, but one who is quick-tempered displays folly.**
> Proverbs 14:29 (NIV)

If we entertain curiosity in this way it will stimulate another conversation within our minds as outlined above, which prevents us from being fully present and authentically *listening* to what they are saying.

Breaking this cycle requires us to leverage curiosity to our advantage. Rather than using curiosity to stimulate diagnosis, we use this curiosity to gain a deeper understanding of our children.

What are they thinking?
What are they saying, experiencing, and feeling?
What do they really mean by _____?

Instead of jumping to these conclusions on our own, we ask our children what they mean and listen as they answer.

Whether it is a word, a statement, or body language that piques our curiosity, we must allow it to prompt further exploration with effective questions and then listen. For example:

- "I want to understand. Can you tell me more about _____?"
- "You mentioned that you don't feel loved. Can you tell me more about that?"
- "I am curious; you mentioned _____. What does that mean to you?"
- "That seems to stir deep emotion in you. Can you tell me what you're feeling right now?"
- "You said _____. Tell me more about that?"
- "You look troubled. Can you tell me what's going on?"

Keying in on what makes us curious and then asking our child to tell us what that means to them, instead of trying to figure it out ourselves, leads us toward a true understanding of what they are thinking, feeling, and/or experiencing. It further prevents us from falling into the trap of diagnosing or misunderstanding what they truly intend.

There is a relational bonus for us with this approach; we communicate to our children that we are not willing to jump to incorrect conclusions or hasty judgments about them, and further, we make relationship a priority. Even if I do not agree with my child, I can still love them unconditionally and listen to fully understand them and where they are coming from.

Leveraging curiosity in this way creates a new conversational pattern.

1. Curiosity leads to,
2. *Asking* which leads to,
3. *Listening* which leads to,
4. *Clarifying* which leads to,
5. *Understanding*.
6. Which *Supports Relationship* and *Growth*.

"The difference between a great listener and a poor listener is found within their ability to manage one critical component - the mind."

Exercise

A. List 5 ways you can demonstrate active listening and become fully present when your child is speaking.

1. Giving them full attention by turning off the television, computer or closing the book.
2.
3.
4.
5.

B. Invite your children to help you become a better listener by offering them the opportunity to observe you 'in action.' Let them know in advance that you would like to spend time with them simply to listen and the topic of conversation will be of their choosing. Practice using curiosity in order to gain greater understanding. When they are speaking, take notice of what makes you curious and then ask something like, "You mentioned _____ tell me more about that."

Do this for 10 or 15 minutes and then take a moment to reflect on your conversation.

- How did following your curiosity to gain greater understanding affect your conversation?
- How did your child respond?
- What could following your curiosity to gain understanding do within all of your conversations?

A New Commitment

Most communication training focuses upon speaking so others will listen, but I firmly believe that our time would be better used in learning to listen so that others will speak. If you would like to make that commitment today yourself, you can right here and right now. Fill in the sentence below and sign after it signifying the commitment to authentic listening that you are making today.

Today, _____ (date), I sacrificially commit myself to be fully present for my children. I will treat our conversations as sacred and refuse to allow anything to distract me from giving my full, undivided attention to them.

_____
Signed

Congratulations, you have taken a great step forward with your listening. I expect that as you fulfill this commitment you will greatly improve your ability to *Support Relationship through Understanding*. Both you and your child will be better for it.

Chapter 10

Clarifying

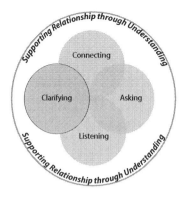

Supporting Relationship through Understanding

Connecting

Clarifying   Asking

Listening

> "When my parents ask me what I mean by something I said and then take the time to really listen to me, it helps me know that they really want to understand me and that makes me feel good inside."
>
> Angela, 14

"That isn't what I meant at all; you're always jumping to conclusions!"

Can this accusation be avoided in parenting?

Absolutely!

Clarification is the linchpin of understanding, bringing the issue or topic of conversation into sharp focus. When used frequently during our conversations we ensure that we understand exactly what our child is saying, and we can avoid the dreaded accusation, "That isn't what I meant at all, you're always jumping to conclusions!" *Clarifying* ensures that there is a mutual understanding between us and our child and maintains health within our conversations together.

Understanding is foundational to healthy relationship. How many times have we come to the realization that an argument, disagreement, or conflict has been the result of a misunderstanding? These unfortunate experiences serve as powerful reminders that we have sometimes mistakenly presumed we understood our child, when in fact we didn't.

"Clarification is the linchpin of understanding, bringing the issue or topic of conversation into sharp focus."

The reality is, far too often within families, misunderstandings are the fuel for relational conflict. *Clarifying* brings the conversation into clear focus, and prevents unnecessary relational conflict due to misunderstandings.

Giving our Children Permission to Correct Us

"That isn't what I meant at all; what I mean is . . ." It is important to give our children permission to correct us when we are wrong. Remember, they are the experts on what they are thinking, feeling and experiencing, so they have the information we need. It is imperative that we listen to understand, and when we are unsure of anything we clarify, and then wait for them to confirm it. *Clarifying* is like the 'checkpoint' in a conversation, it is the moment of truth, where we ask for confirmation on whether or not we are truly understanding what they intend to communicate.

> **"Far too often within families, mis-understandings are the fuel for relational conflict."**

Giving our child permission to say "No, that is not what I meant; what I meant was . . ." and *listening* as they correct us, tells our child that;

> we value relationship,
> we are approachable,
> we truly want to understand them,
> we give them the benefit of the doubt, and
> we don't always have to be right.

Ultimately, we're saying to them, "I value and respect you as a person, and truly want to understand what you are saying, thinking, and feeling. If I ever misunderstand you, you have permission to correct me." This is an incredible way to support a healthy relationship and can prevent fostering the attitude that Roberta now holds about her parents.

> "I don't even bother trying to open up to my parents anymore. They just jump to conclusions and then begin to rant about why I should or shouldn't do this or that. I think they are more concerned with their 'rules' than they are about me as a person. They never give me the opportunity to fully explain my side of a story, or see my point of view. So why should I bother opening up to them? I know my friends understand me, so when I have something I need to talk about, I just go to one of them."
>
> Roberta, 15

A true understanding can only be attained when both the parent and child step away from conversation knowing without a doubt that they are in agreement as to what the other intended. As a general rule, never assume you fully understand what your child is saying until they have confirmed it. There is something reassuring in those simple words, "Yes, that is exactly what I mean."

In the course of conversation, simply make it a habit to clarify, ensuring that what is being heard is truly what the child intends. Yes, it does take a little more time, but having the assurance that we truly understand is a relatively simple way to communicate love and minimize unnecessary relational conflict.

Exercise

Take a moment now and write down three additional statements or questions that you can use as *clarifying* 'check points' in conversation. In this way you will be prepared the next time you need to confirm that you understand what your child is saying.

- "If I understand you correctly, you mean . . . . Is that right?"
- "So, what you're saying is . . . . Is that what you mean?"
-
-
-

Bringing Clarity to the Conversation

Conversations can go downhill fast and misunderstandings get out of control, simply because we do not interpret information in the same way. Each of us has different perceptual filters through which we interpret information; our history, upbringing, culture, personality and experiences all contribute to the way we personally perceive and interpret words. Great care needs to be taken in conversation to ensure that we truly do understand what the other is saying, and *clarifying* helps us do this.

When there is clarity and understanding it brings greater depth and power to our coaching conversations. Let me illustrate for you how *clarifying* can help us gain a true understanding of what someone means and bring greater depth to the conversation by sharing the following coaching conversation with you.

"Conversations can go downhill fast and misunderstandings get out of control, simply because we do not interpret information in the same way."

Clarifying Within a Coaching Conversation

Background

Trevor is a college student in his second year of studies as he pursues a business degree. His studies have taken him almost two thousand kilometers away from family and friends. Despite the fact he has moved away from everything familiar, he is a very outgoing young man and has developed some healthy friendships quickly. Although he misses home, he has indicated that he loves his new surroundings, his friends and school. As the conversation continues he opens up and begins sharing that the workload is starting to get to him; the weight of his studies, practical work placements and time demands have been increasing and then he makes the following statement:

> "It feels like I am reaching the end of my emotional, social, and sanity ropes. The past couple of weeks have been really rough and I'm just trying to keep pushing myself forward."

This comment piqued my curiosity, but rather than allow it to spur my mind toward diagnosing, I allowed it to bring more information out in the open by asking a *clarifying* question.

"Never assume you understand what another person is saying. Always make it a practice to *clarify*."

Coaching Conversation	Observation
"That's a pretty significant statement, Trevor. Can you help me understand what you mean by that?"	Asking a *clarifying* question.
"The biggest part of the stress for me is my long distance relationship with Samantha. We are hitting some communication speed bumps and it is affecting my emotional state more than I would like it to."	As Trevor shares he reveals a relational issue with his girlfriend that otherwise would have been missed entirely. *Clarifying* in this way gave Trevor the freedom to open up and share what was really troubling him.
"In what way?"	
"There is a part of me that just wants to be able to see her and actually have a relationship with her that does not rely on technology to talk to or see each other. Both of us are very busy people, too, so that makes it even more difficult to talk and it's taking a toll on me. I've discovered that I don't really know how to balance life here and my relationships back home. So everything suffers. It's hard to keep a relational mind set all the time, because I am so focused on pouring everything I have into school and my work placement. To be honest, our relationship takes a 'when I get to it' mentality. Samantha and I have talked about this and it just made things more awkward."	*Asking* and continuing to *listen* opened conversation and took it to a greater depth than initially anticipated. That's the power of coaching.

Following my curiosity provided Trevor with the opportunity to share what he was truly feeling and gave me a clear understanding of what he was experiencing. The conversation became powerful because what was lying beneath the surface of his words was brought out in the open through *clarifying*. It allowed him to share what was really important to him which led to my being able to support his growth in this area through coaching. Over the next several weeks we engaged in coaching conversations through which he explored the possibility of restoring balance to his life. He committed to value based boundaries to maintain health in his relationships, work, and studies.

One comment that stands out in my mind as we concluded our coaching appointments was this:

> "Greg, just having you there to listen, knowing I had the freedom to share
> my heart and talk out loud has been very beneficial for me."

Clarifying is the linchpin of understanding, bringing the issue or topic of conversation into sharp focus. It provides us with the necessary information to move forward and ensure that we truly understand our children. *Supporting Relationship* in this way captures the heart of our child, strengthens relationship and opens the door toward *Supporting* their *Growth* by coaching the deeper issues within their lives.

Exercise

Begin practicing the *clarifying* technique in conversation with others this week. Don't settle for assuming that you understand what is intended, ensure you understand by *clarifying*. Soon it will become natural for you and as you grow in understanding you will gain a greater appreciation of those around you. Intentionally ask *clarifying* questions and at the end of each conversation take a few moments and reflect.

- What impact did *clarifying* have upon this conversation?
- What did you find taking place within your heart and mind as you intentionally sought understanding through the *clarifying* technique?
- What did you observe about the other individuals you were speaking with as you sought understanding through clarification?
- How did they respond?

Chapter

11

Supporting Relationship through Understanding:
Model in Action

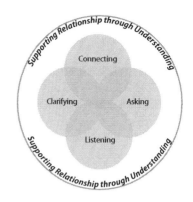

Now that you have observed each discipline within the *Supporting Relationship through Understanding* model; *Connecting, Asking, Listening and Clarifying,* are you ready to put them all together? Let's begin and see what change this brings within our relationships and understanding of one another.

Scenario 1

The first story involves a dad and daughter as they discuss issues surrounding her schoolwork. At this point the daughter's schoolwork is not being completed as Dad would expect. Growing tired of feeling as though he has to 'nag' his daughter to get the desired results, he seeks to gain an understanding of what is going on within her that prevents her from doing the necessary work.

Let's watch as Dad gains a greater understanding of his daughter by *Connecting, Asking, Listening* and *Clarifying*. Notice how *Understanding* changes Dad's perspective of the situation which strengthens their relationship together.

"By wisdom a house is built, and through *UNDERSTANDING* it is established; through knowledge its rooms are filled with rare and beautiful treasures."
Proverbs 24:3-4
(NIV)

Coaching Conversation	Observation
"Do you have a few minutes so we can talk together about something?"	Dad seeks to *connect* by *asking* if she has time to speak together. This gives his daughter a sense of control in the situation. Further, he states what the conversation will be about, and seeks to *connect* relationally by identifying himself as a 'nag.'
"Sure."	
"I would like to talk about your schoolwork. To be honest, I am tired of always fighting with you and nagging you about it. I really don't want to be a nag."	
"Yeah, I am tired of fighting too, Dad."	
"I am just wondering if you can help me understand what's going on with you and your home work. Looking from the outside it seems like you don't care, but I know you better than that and wonder what is really going on."	Dad shares that he desires to understand and states what her actions appear to be from the outside looking in. He affirms his daughter by stating what he sees as 'out of character' for her, which appeals to the relationship they share.
"Can I be honest with you? Will you promise you won't get mad or upset?"	Daughter asks for conditions before proceeding and Dad agrees, again giving her control in this conversation and she begins to open up.
"Yes, of course I promise. And if it looks like I am going to, I give you permission to let me know immediately and call a 'time out.'"	
"OK, deal. I really do care about school, probably more than you realize. It may not be as much as you care about it, but I do care, really. It's just I like to do my homework my own way, when I want to. Not how and when you expect me to."	
"Can you elaborate on that some more?"	Dad seeks to *understand* what she is meaning by asking her to elaborate more.
"Well, as soon as I walk through the door from school the first thing I hear is 'Don't forget your homework; you have to get that done before you do anything else!' You constantly remind me that homework should be first priority, because if I don't get my homework done, I will get bad grades, and if I get bad grades I won't get into college or university. Then if I don't get into college or university I'll end up like my cousin flippin' burgers in some burger joint and, of course, you don't want that."	Dad models *self control* while the daughter shares her perspective. He does well and refrains from becoming defensive.
"Wow, is that really what I sound like?"	
"Yes Dad, that is what you sound like to me. The funny thing is, I know you do it because you care, but when you do this; it makes me feel worse and like I don't want to do my homework at all."	Daughter confirms this is how she feels about the situation.
"I am really sorry that I have made you feel that way. I do want what is best for you and that's why I asked to talk with you today. Can you tell me what I can do to support and encourage you with your studies?"	Dad empathizes with her and apologizes. This is a huge step in the right direction for relationship. He continues by asking his daughter to share what support she believes she

"What I need the most is to come home from school and just kick back for a while before doing my homework. I've just spent the whole day at school, with teachers, students, books and such and it's nice just to break away from that for a bit before jumping back in."

"When you say you would like a 'break before jumping back into your work' do you mean you'd like some time to unwind first and then you'd do your homework?"

"Yeah, that's exactly what I mean. I know you like me to come home and immediately do my homework so the night is free, but I really need some down time between school and homework."

"OK, that sounds reasonable and as I think about this, it makes sense. I didn't take into consideration at all that you might need a break after school. Now that I think about it, when I come home from work, the last thing I want to do is jump back into another work project. Even I like to unwind a bit first."

"Thanks for saying that Dad, that means a lot to me."

"You're very welcome. Thank you for being open and honest with me. I can see your point of view now."

needs. This affirms that he wants to support, but allows her to set up the parameters of that support. This is a good step because our children often do know what support they want from us.

Dad *clarifies* once again and will await confirmation or correction from his daughter.

Daughter confirms that he does understand correctly.

Understanding has brought a different perspective for Dad, and he takes another step by admitting he had not considered this before. Making himself vulnerable this way increases their relational bond.

Daughter affirms Dad's comments and expresses appreciation for them.

Once understanding is established it makes possible a transition toward *Supporting Growth* through coaching with the *EASE* model.

Reflection

- In what way did *understanding* change Dad's perspective on the homework situation?
- How did taking the time to coach this potentially volatile subject disarm conflict and make it productive?
- In what ways do you recognize that their relationship was strengthened?

Coaching with the *Supporting Relationship through Understanding* Model allowed Dad to maintain a healthy posture during this conversation with his daughter. He *asked* effective questions and authentically *listened* to his daughter as she shared her perspective on the issue. Dad *clarified* when necessary which allowed his daughter to verbally confirm that he understood her correctly. Throughout the conversation the daughter was affirmed and left feeling better about herself and her father because understanding had given Dad a different perspective, and he now related to her need to unwind. This process *Supported* health in *Relationship* and made possible an opportunity to transition to *Supporting Growth* by *Exploring the Possibilities* of how she could care for her homework in a way that honors both Dad and herself.

Scenario 2

Supporting Relationship through Understanding is most commonly a conversational process, but as our next story illustrates it can be initiated because of body language that piques our curiosity. We want to leverage our curiosity to gain *understanding* by *asking*, then *listening*, rather than allowing curiosity to stimulate our minds toward false assumptions. The mom in the following story followed her curiosity well as she sought to gain understanding through *Connecting*, *Asking*, *Listening* and *Clarifying*.

Watch how Mom connects with her son and asks questions in a way that opens her son up in conversation.

> **"My dear brothers and sisters, take note of this: Everyone should be quick to listen, slow to speak and slow to become angry, because human anger does not produce the righteousness that God desires."**
> James 1:19-20
> (NIV)

A Mother's Story

"Four months ago our family was thrust into a major life transition. We are in our forties. Having worked in the same field for over 20 years we suddenly found ourselves unemployed and thrust into a new phase of life and work. My parents graciously invited us to move into their home until we were 're-established' but that meant moving away from friends and all that was familiar to us. After discussing this as a family we agreed that it would be the best thing for us to do so we sold our home, and moved in with my parents.

We relocated with a great deal of uncertainty about what this change would bring into our lives and hoped that our children would be OK during the transition. We made sure we spent extra time with them to help them out. Things went smoothly for a while, but after three months something happened that concerned me. One evening, right out of the blue, my son grew noticeably disturbed. As any young man does, he tried to hide it and 'casually' left the room. Well, you know me, a Mom, if my 'baby' is hurting, I am hurting and I wanted to know what was going on within him. It was hard, but I managed to reign in my runaway thoughts, as I waited to see if he would return. Several moments passed and realizing he wasn't going to return, I casually excused myself and made my way upstairs toward his bedroom.

Quietly climbing the stairs I could hear the sound of books, and cd's being tossed and knocked over. With that I could hardly contain myself and I whispered a prayer, 'Lord I don't know what is going on with Randy, and my mind wants to race to the worst places. Please Lord, let me keep my thoughts under control and give me wisdom to know what to ask, and when to keep my mouth shut. 'Lord, may you allow him to be willing to speak with me and when he does, help me listen and have a heart of understanding.'

I knocked gently on the door. There was a brief silence followed by some shuffling around, then I heard, 'Yes?'"

Coaching Conversation	Observation

"May I come in, Randy?" I asked softly and waited for permission to enter.

"Just give me a minute, Mom," he responded. After a few moments the door cracked open and he invited me in and flopped onto his bed. I nestled into his desk chair and just looked at him for a moment. My heart ached as I could see the pain etched upon his face. Not knowing what was taking place within his heart and mind, I ventured out and asked,

Asking permission to come in honors Randy and helps him maintain a sense of control in this situation.

"Randy, it looked as though you were upset when you left the room downstairs; is everything OK?"

"I'll be OK, Mom. It's really no big deal."

Mom looks to connect and acknowledges that she noticed something when he left the room.

"Really? No big deal, eh? Can I say something about that?"

"Yeah, sure. Whatever."

Mom *asks* permission to share her perspective.

"From where I am sitting, it does look like a big deal. You looked troubled when you left the family room, and what I see coming in here, well, it looks as though you've been throwing things around. I know you better than that. Randy, there must be something going on to make you react like this. So tell me, is everything OK, or is there something else going on?"

Mom takes time to paint a picture here of what it looks like from her perspective.

"Yeah, well, I guess you could say everything isn't OK."

"Well?"

"Well, what?"

Randy affirms mom's perception.

"If you want, I could sit here and guess what it is, but you know me, I'd probably just guess wrong. So, am I going to guess what's wrong, or are you going to help me understand what is going on?"

"You probably would just sit here and guess, wouldn't you?"

"Yes, but that's only because I love you."

Mom continues to probe in a light hearted way, hoping to benefit from their relationship by encouraging him to open up and share what's going on.

"Well, you're right, something is wrong. At first I thought this was just a feeling that would pass, but it just keeps getting worse as time goes by and I find myself growing angry."

Randy begins to open up.

"OK. Go on."

"To be completely honest with you, I just don't feel valued; it's like no one really cares and I am not respected anymore."

Mom refrains from jumping in and simply *asks* him to continue talking.

Reflection

Pause for just a moment and connect with what you are thinking.
- How would you respond to this comment from Randy? What would you say?

- Take a moment and write down, in the space provided, what you think may be causing Randy to feel this way.

Once you are finished writing your thoughts down, continue with the conversation.

Coaching Conversation	Observation
"I'm very sorry to hear that; that's not a good feeling at all. Can you help me understand what has contributed to this feeling?" "Well, it's just since we moved. Everything was fine before, I felt like you and Dad respected me and all, but something is different now. I'm not sure why, but I got thinking about it downstairs, and I just needed to get away and think." *"Can you tell me what's different?"* "Ahhh, well, I am not sure how to say it, really." *"Oh? You know you can say anything you like. Nothing you say is going to change my love for you. Just go ahead and we'll work through it once it's out in the open."* "Well, when we first moved, I figured it was just because of the stress of the changes we were going through. You know, no job, retraining and living with Nana and Poppa. So I didn't give it much thought, but it's been building and building and I guess tonight it just got to me." *"What is the 'it' that you are referring to?"* "You know how before, when we were at home and we were making decisions and stuff ..." *"Yes."* "You and Dad would include us in the process, ask our thoughts and opinions on the matter." *"Yes."* "Then you'd always ask us to take time and pray about all that we talked about. Then we'd get back together and talk again, then make our decision together?"	Mom empathizes with Randy asking if he can help her to understand. Mom asks, then sits back to *listen*, allowing him to share without interruption. She follows her curiosity here and asks him to share about 'what's different' now. He hesitates but Mom affirms that he has permission to say anything he likes and she'll maintain her love for him. 'It' is undefined at this point and continues to pique Mom's curiosity. She seeks understanding by *asking* what 'it' is.

"Yes, I remember all of that."

"Well, since we moved, you guys are different. Instead of having our regular family meetings it seems like you just make all of the decisions for us. It's like all of a sudden, our opinion doesn't count and we don't matter anymore. I know Dad has been preoccupied with schooling and more training and stuff, but somehow in all of this, us kids seem to have been forgotten. We're still here, we're still part of the family and when you two don't include us, it hurts."

"Oh, Randy I am so sorry. I didn't even realize that Dad and I were so caught up with all of this, that we were making you feel this way. Do you think we're too busy for you now, is that it?"

"No Mom, it's not that I think you're too busy for me. You guys have been pretty good with that kind of thing and have spent a lot of time with us throughout this move. It's more about the decisions that are being made. We used to do that as a family, each of us having input, but lately that's not the case. You seem to be making all the decisions for the family on your own, and it's like our opinion doesn't matter anymore."

"I'm sorry, honey. I should have picked up on that earlier. So you're saying you felt respected when you were involved in the decision making process and lately we just haven't included you and the others in our decisions. And because of that it seems like your opinion doesn't matter to us. Do I understand correctly now?"

"Yes, that is exactly how I feel. I'm sorry Mom, I don't mean to hurt you, but I feel as though I don't really matter anymore and wonder what happened to us as a family."

"Don't worry about that, honey. It's more important that these things are openly talked about. I appreciate your transparency; otherwise I would never have understood what you were really thinking and why you were upset. Can I make a suggestion here?"

"Sure."

"Can we take some time together with Dad, and the other kids and just talk about all of this. If you're feeling this way, the others might be, too, and I think it would be important to get back on track as a family."

"Sure Mom, that'd be OK."

Now the heart of the issue comes to the surface.

Mom does a great job of *self control/ management* here and doesn't take offense or get defensive. Instead she continues to *listen* as he shares so she can gain a true understanding of what is on his mind.

Mom identifies with Randy's hurt here, and *clarifies* to see if she understands correctly.

Randy indicates that she doesn't understand yet and restates his concern for her so she can understand.

Clarifying is important to ensure we understand exactly what our children are thinking.

Mom restates again to ensure that she does understand this time and *asks* for confirmation from Randy.

Randy confirms her understanding and even apologizes if he has hurt her in any way by sharing so openly.

Mom acknowledges and affirms his transparency, highlighting the importance of having these kinds of issues out in the open so they can be worked through in a healthy manner.

She then *asks* if she can make a suggestion, again, honoring Randy and allowing him to maintain a sense of control in the conversation.

Scenario 3

The final story is a humorous conversation between our 11 year old daughter Hannah and I. You will quickly recognize that this conversation illustrates well the fact that we perceive and understand words through different perceptual filters which can create some humorous misunderstandings.

Hannah had been saving money for a couple of years to make a very special purchase. She desired to have and care for a dog of her own and set her sights upon a miniature Dachshund. This past summer she reached her savings goal and had shown to both Lynn and I that she was responsible enough to care for a dog of her own. Upon receiving our go ahead with the purchase, she searched for and located a breeder, who coincidentally had puppies born on her birthday. Lynn helped her make the arrangements to see the puppy and the following conversation quickly followed:

Observe how easy it is for simple words to be interpreted differently which can lead to misunderstandings.

Coaching Conversation	Observation
"Dad, if I like the color of the dachshund, and the parents are good-natured, I am going to hold the puppy"	Hannah connects with me by initiating the conversation.
"That sounds great, honey, but can I ask a question?"	Slightly confused I ask permission to *ask* a question.
"Sure."	I *clarify*.
"When we visit the family who has the puppy, are you intending on holding it first or making the decision about buying it first, and then holding it?"	
"Definitely make the decision first."	I am still confused.
"That's interesting, honey. I thought you would be interested in holding the puppy first and seeing	I state how I perceive she would move forward. Hoping that she will correct

if you like it, and it likes you, before making the decision."

"Yes, holding it would be good for that, Dad, but that is not what I mean."

"Alrighty then, can you help me understand what you mean?"

With strong emphasis she now responds. "If I like the color and the parents seem to have a good nature, I am going to hold it, so I can pick it up when it is ready to leave its mommy! Do you understand what I mean now?"

I laughed, and although I wanted to tease her a bit by pretending that I still didn't understand, I resisted and asked, *"Do you mean you're going to put a deposit on it, so they will 'hold' it for you to come back and get it when it's ready to leave its mom?"*

"Yeah, that's what I mean!"

Again, I laughed. *"OK, now I understand. I thought it was a bit strange that you wouldn't even hold onto the puppy when you went to see it."*

"Don't be silly, Daddy."

me and help me understand what she is meaning. Hannah states that what I understand 'hold' to mean, is not what she means at all.

I *ask* again for clarification.

As I *listen* carefully, the emphasis in her tone clues me in. I think she means putting a deposit on the puppy to hold it for her.

I *clarify* again by restating what I think she is saying and then *listen* for her to affirm or correct my understanding.

Hannah confirms that Daddy finally understands.

Reflection

This humorous dialogue illustrates how easy it is for people to be speaking, even using the same words, yet completely misunderstand the other's meaning.

- What can that story teach us about the importance of understanding in our conversations?
- What one thing will you commit to in order to ensure you understand your children?

Personally I prefer to experience misunderstandings like these as opposed to the misunderstanding that fuel relational conflict. You and I both know how easily they take place. Often the relational strain we have experienced personally or witnessed in ministry has been caused by a misunderstanding of some sort.

Supporting Relationship through Understanding must be a priority for us if we are to foster health within our relationship and most naturally transition to supporting our children's growth. Remember we are emulating God's strategy with us as His children. Focus upon *Supporting Relationship* first. Then, as we earn our children's trust they will most naturally open up and give us permission to touch the deeper areas of their hearts and *Support their Growth* by *Exploring Possibilities, Assessing Desire, Securing Commitment* and *Encouraging* their *Progress.*

Reflection

Take a few moments and reflect upon all you have read to this point about *Supporting Relationship through Understanding.*

- How could the *Supporting Relationship through Understanding* model add value to the relationship you have with your children?
- In what way could you apply the understanding model within your parenting today?
- What's one step you will take today that will set you on the path of *Supporting a Relationship through Understanding* with your child?

Chapter

12

Part 3
Transitioning from Supporting Relationship to Supporting Growth

"Supporting Growth involves understanding where our child is, knowing where they want to go, and giving them the support they need to get there."

Pro-Active Parent Coaching Model

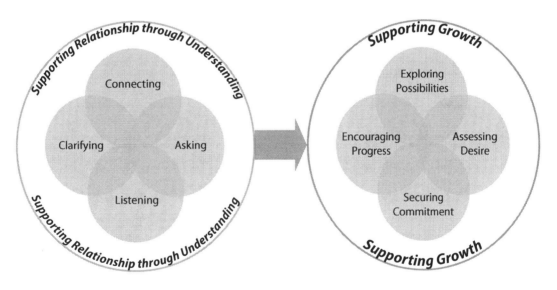

"My parents have coached me for a few years now and it seems as though we are working together instead of against one another. I see some of my friends and their parents, fighting against each other, and feel lucky with how my own Mom and Dad work with me. They have let me make my own decisions, and even some decisions that hurt me for a bit. But, overall, I feel much better about myself and have a new respect for my parents and the way they parent me."

Tom, 16

> **"Although every coaching conversation may not focus upon a growth goal, every conversation does support relationship."**

Everything rises and falls upon relationship. Our children's openness and transparency with us flows within the context of healthy relationship. The ability to capture their hearts is within our reach when we seek to understand and respect them for who they are and who they are becoming. Their willingness to open up and give us permission to touch the deeper matters of their lives and support their growth through coaching largely depends upon the health and strength of our relationship. For this very reason, the primary purpose of the parent coaching model in this book focuses on establishing and *Supporting a Relationship through Understanding*.

When we experience the rich relational connection that putting the heart, skills, and disciplines of coaching into practice, it may be tempting to stop here, believing we have arrived and simply enjoy the rich relational connection we are experiencing. But, this is just the beginning! Our children need and deserve more from us if they are going to understand their role in History, and be prepared for life beyond our homes. We must now transition to supporting their growth. Our love for our children, coupled with our concern for their wellbeing and future compels us to do so.

Throughout our journey into the coaching process we will enjoy many rich and wonderful conversations with our children. Although every coaching conversation may not focus upon a growth goal, every conversation does *support relationship*. For the purpose of the next few chapters, we will turn our attention toward *Supporting Growth*, which, interestingly enough, also continues to foster, strengthen and *support relationship*.

P.O.P. Principle of Pro-Active Parent Coaching

Pray for God to bring the people and experiences into our child's life that will foster their desire for growth and change.
Observe and keep an eye open for teachable moments within their lives.
Position ourselves as coaches for our children when they want to talk.

Natural Transitions

Supporting Relationship through Understanding is an enjoyable component of coaching and can be experienced very early within our child's life. When practiced from an early age it establishes a regular rhythm of healthy communication between us and our children. Conversations that might otherwise seem odd or unrealistic to some people (which you may have wondered about with the opening conversation between Katelyn and I in chapter 1) become normal, natural and expected, helping us to truly understand what our children are thinking, feeling and experiencing. This is what gives life to our coaching relationship.

More often than not, the relationship we establish with our children during their development characterizes the relationship we will carry on with them throughout life. If we have always done for them, or told them what to do, we will tend to do the same after they leave home. But, if we have empowered them through coaching while they are young, we will establish a healthy interdependent relationship and will naturally transition from parent coach to peer coach as they launch into *responsible adulthood*. The benefit of coaching is seen in the fact that this makes our children's transition into adulthood much easier for both us and them. They are better prepared because they have been equipped with essential life skills prior to leaving home, and parents are better prepared because they have already begun the process of 'letting go' in a healthy manner by releasing responsibility and giving more freedom through coaching.

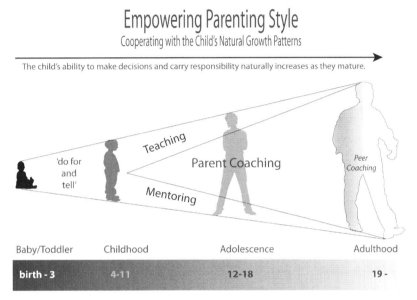

The Internal Challenge

Supporting Growth is as exciting as *Supporting a Relationship through Understanding* is enjoyable. Within this stage of coaching we truly recognize our children's growing ability, and the potential that God has deposited within them. Giving greater freedom, allowing them to make decisions and releasing responsibility can be an incredibly enlightening experience for us. But, this is where the rubber meets the road. Up to this point our coaching conversations have focused upon relationship. Now our focus intentionally shifts to *Supporting Growth*. This will take greater discipline and internal fortitude to resist jumping in, rescuing our children or sheltering them from all the pain they may experience. We make a conscious decision to surrender absolute control, and this can be easier said than done.

> **"What is difficult for some parents is allowing their children to keep responsibility, after it has been given."**

What is difficult for some parents is allowing their children to keep responsibility, after it has been given. Some want to control every aspect of their child's growth and when this happens it creates an internal tension, frustrating their healthy growth and development and ultimately affecting relationship in a negative way.

As we move forward to *Supporting Growth* let's take one last look at the *Limiting Parenting Style*, to *'do for and tell.'*

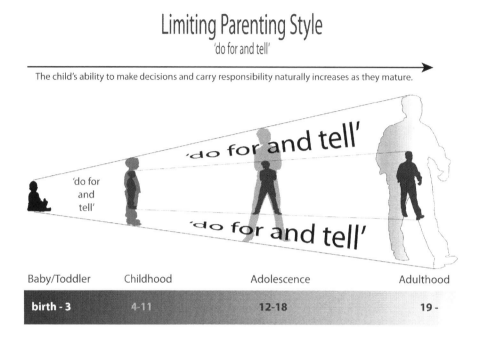

Limiting Parenting Style
'do for and tell'

The child's ability to make decisions and carry responsibility naturally increases as they mature.

Baby/Toddler	Childhood	Adolescence	Adulthood
birth - 3	4-11	12-18	19 -

Take notice of the outside lines: these represent our children's *Natural Growth Patterns* and their increasing ability to carry responsibility and make decisions on their own. The inside lines represent where we have limited them by neglecting to give them freedom that corresponds with their growing ability to manage it. Take notice of the distance between the lines. This distance measures the tension within our relationship and/or the energy compelling our child to become independent of us in order to gain the freedom they need to exercise their growing ability.

Supporting Growth moves away from the *'Limiting Parenting Style'* and begins giving greater freedom and responsibility to our children in accordance to their ability.

Pro-Active Parent Coaches believe:
- The earlier our children are allowed to take responsibility, the more likely they are going to be to take responsibility.
- The easier it is for them to take responsibility, the more likely they are going to be to take responsibility.
- The higher their motivation toward responsibility, the more likely they are going to be to take responsibility.
- The more support and encouragement they receive while carrying responsibility, the more likely they will be to take responsibility in the future.

It is our heart as Pro-Active Parent Coaches to intentionally *E.A.S.E.* our children into growth and responsibility as they mature toward responsible adulthood, not simply cut them loose at a pre-determined point in time. What our children learn throughout their growth and development increases their resourcefulness and ability to manage their lives throughout life.

While, it's true that *Pro-Active Parent Coaching* intentionally focuses upon our children's growth, *Supporting Growth* is much more comprehensive than simply performance goals. We can effectively coach our children through a vast array of growth experiences; from issues of self esteem, relationships, decisions, life purpose, calling, dream development, schooling, values, self awareness and much, much more.

Supporting Growth

Supporting Growth is a relatively easy process through which we turn our focus from understanding a topic, issue or concern toward supporting our children's growth in that area. By *Exploring Possibilities, Assessing Desire, Securing Commitment* and *Encouraging Progress* we provide our children with the necessary support and encouragement they need on their growth journey.

By way of example, I would like to illustrate how this process works by sharing a couple of coaching conversations I had with our second daughter, Hannah.

Background

Very early in Hannah's life we recognized a generous spirit growing within her. Often she would approach Lynn and I for our approval to give something away to someone she desired to bless, whether it was a toy, or something that she had made for them. In light of this growing realization, we were not surprised at the following conversation, but it provided a great opportunity to Support her Growth in developing creative ways to earn money.

In October of 2009 Hannah approached me and shared her desire to give everyone Christmas gifts that year, with one significant stipulation; she wanted to pay for them herself. Watch as this coaching conversation unfolds, and notice how I honor Hannah's desire and *Support her Growth* through coaching.

Coaching Conversation	Observation
"Dad, I've been thinking that this year I would like to buy everyone Christmas presents by myself." *"Really, you know you don't have to do that, right?* "Yeah, I know, but I'd really like to." *"That's very thoughtful of you. I guess you are growing up, aren't you! Do you know what you want to purchase?"* "Well, over the past little while I've been looking at stuff at the stores that I think everyone would like. I have a rough idea of how much the gifts would cost me."	Hannah takes great pleasure in giving gifts and ensuring that they are personalized. Not wanting to strip her of this opportunity I engage in conversation about how she can do this. I affirm her thoughtfulness and ask a direct question about how much money she will need. The growth opportunity here for Hannah is taking responsibility for purchasing gifts on her own, and growing in her ability

"OK."

"I want to spend between $15.00 and $20.00 on each person in our family, so I will need around $150.00."

"That's very generous, Hannah."

"Thank you. But there's one problem."

"What's that?"

"I am not sure how I can get that much money."

"Oh? Well I might be able to help you with that. Do you mind if I ask you some questions and maybe we can come up with some possibilities on how you can earn enough money?"

"Yeah, that would be great."

"As you think about this, what are some things you could do that would help you earn the money you need?"

"Well, we could do a yard sale."

"That's one possibility. What else could you do?"

"Umm, well, selling my pictures online hasn't done a lot yet."

"True, so there must be another possibility. What would it be?"

"Umm, I could make crafts to sell."

"Yup, that's a good idea too. Can you think of anything else?"

"Hmm, I'm not sure, Dad."

"OK, let's see if we can think of at least one more. What is the thing we haven't thought of yet?"

- Silence -

"Ohh, I could do yard work, raking leaves, and stuff, for people around the subdivision."

"That's great! You're doing very well at this. Is there anything else hiding somewhere in that mind of yours that we can pull out?"

- Silence -

"Umm, no I can't think of anything else, Dad."

"That's OK, you have thought of some great ideas here; would you like to consider them now?"

"Sure."

"You have thought of making crafts to sell, having a yard sale, and doing some yard work like raking leaves and such. So when you consider

to create possibilities for herself in relation to earning money.

Hannah's objective is stated: $150.00. Although in my mind I think that she is going to talk about money, I let her state what the issue is. This ensures that she is in control of the conversation, but also prevents me from jumping to incorrect conclusions.

Asking permission keeps Hannah in control of the conversation and where she wants to go with it.

She begins to *Explore Possibilities*.

Asking 'what else,' will put more options on the table, but also stretches her thinking a little beyond the obvious, or what she may have already considered herself prior to speaking with me.

I want to encourage her to stretch her thinking, this is often where our child will break out of the box and tap into their creativity. I allow silence so she can think.

I affirm her ideas and ability to generate options.

Begin turning our attention toward *Assessing Desire*. The key here is for me to zero in on what she is most excited about working on. That is what I will ask for commitment on. I restate the possibilities she thought of and ask which she would really like to do.

these possibilities, what would you really like to do?"

"Hmm, the yard sale is pretty easy, but I don't think I'd make much at that. The last one we had, I only made a few dollars and that isn't going to do. You know, I think the best thing for me to do would be to make the crafts."

"OK, what attracts you to the crafts?"

"Well, there are a couple of things. I already have a lot of photos taken, and I wonder if I could use them in some way to make a craft to sell. Mom mentioned that a group is getting together and renting a booth at the mall to sell stuff at in November. We could join with them and the crafts I make could be sold there."

"That's a good idea! So what kind of craft do you think you can make with the photos?"

"Well, we could make calendars out of them and sell them to the people."

"Yes, that sounds good. Is there anything else you can think of?"

"We could also make some greeting cards and maybe even bookmarks."

"Great ideas, is this something you would like to do?"

"Yes, I would love to do this, it would be fun, and I think I could earn enough money this way, too."

"What, specifically, are you going to do?"

"Well, I want to make money with this so I will need to check out how much it is going to cost to make calendars, cards and bookmarks before I decide which ones I will do for sure. So I guess the first thing I will do is check out the prices of paper and stuff I need, then decide what I will make. When that is done, I'll begin making the stuff right away to take to the mall."

"When do you plan on starting?"

"I'll start this week."

"Great, in what other way can I support you with this project?"

"On our next date day, will you take me to the stores and price out the paper, and materials we will need?"

"Of course I will, that sounds like a great date day to me."

Hannah evaluates the possibilities now.

I continue to *Assess* her *Desire*.

I ask for specifics here, "What kind of craft?"

I *Explore* more *Possibilities*.

Assessing Desire: "I would love to do this," is a strong positive indicator for me that she is motivated to work on this.

To *Support Growth* and ensure action we need to move beyond desire and *Secure Commitment*: What will you do and by when? I do this by *asking* what she will specifically do, and then, when she plans to start.

I offer continued support by asking, "In what other way can I support you?"

Notice I am committed to the process; I want to support her as best I can while not taking responsibility away from her. By doing so, this experience provides her with the greatest learning.

In preparation for our date together, Hannah charted our course: first, we would go to the supply stores to check prices for calendar production and greeting cards, make the decision and purchase the needed materials, and lastly, go to the mall to grab a drink and just chat. All of this sounded like a great time together to me!

"That's a lot of money, Daddy. I think we better look at the price of making greeting cards!" Hannah said softly, as the expense of creating calendars sunk in.

"We can do that honey. Greeting cards I am certain will be less expensive for you to make." Slipping her arm into mine we walked together into the craft center where Hannah's enthusiasm was re-ignited.

Hannah's eyes widened with excitement, "This is a better price for sure! What do you think Daddy?"

I looked at her smiling face, *"Definitely! We can make greeting cards and keep the sale price low for your customers. Is this what you want to do?"*

"Yes, it is!"

"I think you'll do great, Hannah!" With a sense of victory, we loaded the card-stock and envelopes into the shopping cart and headed to the mall for a beverage. Later that evening, Lynn and I helped Hannah put the cards together and box them for the big sale.

As Hannah's parent coach, I used the first three stages of *Supporting Growth* through *E.A.S.E., Exploring Possibilities, Assessing Desire and Securing Commitment.* I asked Hannah to consider her 'dilemma', i.e., of not having enough money for Christmas gifts, and generate possibilities for earning money to buy the gifts she wanted to give. Asking her questions, as opposed to telling her what she could do, allowed Hannah to tap into her own creativity and grow in her ability to think through possibilities. Additionally, these are her own ideas so she will tend to be more motivated toward carrying them out.

When Hannah had thought of several ideas, I moved her to the *Assessing Desire* stage by asking, "So when you consider these possibilities, what would you really like to do?" In this way, I determined what she was most motivated to work on. When that was discovered I moved to *Securing Commitment* by having her tell me exactly what she was going to do and what time frame she would need to accomplish her goals. This is an easy and natural process anyone can use when supporting their children's growth through coaching.

The natural next step for us is the *Encouraging Progress* stage. We want to keep energy high and provide the necessary encouragement that will build motivation within them as they move toward their objectives. Realize that our children, just as we do, sometimes face discouragement and lose focus because of circumstances. *Encouraging Progress* gives us the opportunity to *encourage,* inspiring our children to keep moving forward.

Because Hannah verbalized her commitment, a healthy accountability structure has already been established. This makes further coaching conversations not only possible, but expected. We begin by asking for a progress report and allowing our children to share about what they have accomplished, or learned so far. As we listen, we are instinctively looking for ways to encourage the steps they have already taken toward fulfilling their objective. Remember, even small steps toward their objective are growth markers that need to be acknowledged and celebrated. You may discover, as I did with Hannah, that the objectives are not always met as quickly as they hope for, and we may need to revisit the *E.A.S.E.* model and adjust their course of action if necessary.

After I asked how the sale went, Hannah revealed that her objective was not met. Observe how I encouraged the progress that she had already made, and refocused her upon the objective. This brought encouragement and motivation back to Hannah, to keep moving toward her original objective.

Coaching Conversation	Observation
"So tell me how the sale went today?" "I did OK, I guess. I sold 42 cards, but it doesn't give me enough money to buy the gifts I wanted to give this year." *"That's OK. How much did you make?"* "After I subtract the price of my supplies, I only made $70.00." *"That's awesome, Honey! Think about it: $70.00 has brought you almost to the half way mark. You're doing great! All we have to do now is think of additional ways to sell your cards."* "OK." *"Would you like to do that?"* "Yeah, that'd be great!" *"OK, so what other possibilities can you think of?"* "We could rent a table again and do another Saturday sale." *"That's a good idea. Is there anything else you can think of?"* "I can call family members and ask if they want to buy some of the cards." *"Yes, that's another possibility; see, you're pretty good at coming up with ideas! What else could you do?"* "I'm not sure." *"OK, give it a moment or two; something might come to you."* -silence- *"Have you thought of everything you can?"* "Yes, I can't think of anything else." *"Could I make a couple of suggestions for you to think about?"* "Sure!"	I ask for progress report on the sale, which helps me gain understanding of what took place and how she did overall. Hannah is noticeably discouraged. This is seen in her focus upon what she didn't accomplish, as opposed to what she had already done, and the tone of her voice. I want to redirect her attention to the fact she has almost reached the half way point, and that is great progress. What you cannot hear in reading this conversation is the renewed energy the 'OK' carries with it. Her voice fills with excitement again when she realizes just how much she has already accomplished. This is further emphasized by her positive response to my asking if she wants to revisit the E.A.S.E. model and *Explore Possibilities* once again. This keeps responsibility with Hannah, because I am not 'rescuing' her by offering solutions or giving her money, but allowing her to walk through this process once again. I give Hannah permission to take time and think this through by allowing silence before asking if she is done. I want to see Hannah be as successful as she can be, but her objective isn't my primary focus; what she is learning through this process is.

"Remember, these are just ideas for you to consider, you can choose one of these, or something else if you like. That is completely up to you."

"OK."

"You could approach some of the many craft stores in the area and ask if you can set up a permanent display of your cards in their store."

"That's a good idea, Dad."

"Thank you. We could also post your cards for sale on Daddy's Facebook® account and see if that generates any interest or sales for you."

"Ohhh, I like that too!"

"What do you think about these ideas?"

"I like them. Do you have any more ideas?"

"No, not really. So if you were to look at these possibilities then: renting another table in the mall; calling family members to buy some of the cards; approaching craft stores to put up a display; or posting on Facebook®, what are you most attracted to?"

"Let's post them on Facebook®, I like that idea the best."

"You're sure?"

"Yes, let's do it today!"

"Alright, let's see what happens."

I have a couple of ideas myself and ask permission to share them. Notice I use the term 'could' not 'should' in offering these suggestions.

In making suggestions we must hold our ideas loosely, giving our child the freedom to accept or decline them without feeling bad in any way. In some cases they may need our reassurance that they can dismiss an idea of ours and we'll be fine with that.

Here I am *Assessing Desire*.

I restate the *Possibilities* for her consideration and ask what she is most attracted to?

Her decision is quick and definitive and we *Secure Commitment* with ease.

The beauty of coaching is found in the fact it provides a natural support structure for our children's growth through continued coaching conversations. It's also WIN - WIN. We support our children's growth, and as we do so, they mature in responsibility and their respect for us grows. As a result our relationship with them is strengthened.

The Outcome

"This is an easy and natural process anyone can use when supporting their children's growth through coaching."

I don't want to leave you hanging here, so let me share with you what took place with Hannah's earning objective. Once Hannah made her decision to display the cards for sale on my Facebook® account, we sat together at the computer and created a new photo album. This act in itself was a great time of connection between us that affirmed Lynn's and my support and belief in Hannah's ability, decisions, and growth in this area. Over the next two weeks Hannah sold an additional 85 cards, earning enough money to purchase all the Christmas gifts she desired to give, make a special donation to the church, and continue saving toward a special gift her heart was set upon. Not only that, she reached her objective early, by finishing all of her shopping on November 28th!

What this experience developed within Hannah's character, and what she learned through the process, has greater importance than simply meeting her objective. She had a desire to grow in responsibility with something as simple as giving Christmas gifts on her own. Allowing her to do so affirmed her ability, desire, and generous spirit. It empowered her to stretch and grow in her ability to think creatively and earn money on her own. This has impacted her ability to look at situations, dream of possibilities, and learn to appreciate the small steps toward her goals, realizing that they are not always easily reached.

"It is our heart as pro-active parent coaches to intentionally E.A.S.E. our children into growth and responsibility"

This stage of coaching, *Supporting Growth,* calls our children to;

> commit to action steps
> which creates a tangible process
> toward a desired objective.

This naturally allows us to provide a healthy accountability structure through which we can encourage their progress.

Exercise

Think of a specific "situation" your child is facing in which you would be willing to attempt the '*Explore Possibilities, Assess Desire,* and *Secure Commitment*' process of decision making. Set a specific time to begin speaking with your child about this, and implement the E.A.S.E. model. As you use this method, pay particular attention to what happens within your child and yourself throughout the process. As you reflect, consider the following;

- What did you notice about your child as you refrained from offering solutions and instead asked them to create their own possibilities?
- How did they initially respond to this approach?
- How would you describe your own feelings as you patiently waited for them to come up with possibilities and then gave them freedom to choose what they wanted to do?
- What did you notice happening within your child as you released responsibility in this way?

If this is a new process for you, realize that it may seem a little awkward at the beginning for both yourself and your child. Try your best to keep them responsible for creating possibilities, selecting one to follow, and then committing to see it through.

Focus on Growth not Terminology

Although this is a goal oriented conversation I want to sound a cautionary note here; don't get hung up on terminology. Some children will be excited and motivated toward working on a goal. On the other hand, some children may be turned off by the term *goal*. The key is to understand what terminology our children respond best to and use that.

For instance, if a child responds favorably to the word goal, by all means speak in those terms.

> "What is your goal?"
> > "What progress have you made toward your goal?"

On the other hand, if a child responds better to another term such as, 'objective,' 'dream,' 'desire,' 'achieve,' 'aim,' or even something else, use one of those terms instead. You could easily ask,

> "What is your objective?"
> > "What do you want to achieve?"
> > > "What do you desire?"
> > > > "What do you want to do?"

Exercise

The focus is *Supporting* our children's *Growth*, not *proper terminology*. If we connect with our child by using terminology that they respond to, it will be more enjoyable, and you will experience greater success within the coaching conversation. Consider the following;

- What terms would your child best respond to?
- Take a moment and consider the uniqueness of your own child. In thinking of growth objectives, what terms might turn your child off?
- What might they connect with and relate to the most?

Make a commitment that you will connect with your child based upon their needs, as opposed to insisting upon specific terminology.

A Note on Failure

There is a huge difference between our child failing at something and being a failure. One of the greatest challenges our children will face throughout life is how to work through and process their shortcomings in a healthy and productive manner. Our view of failure will greatly influence our children's view and their ability to learn from and manage it well.

Can I challenge you to consider these occasions as an incredible opportunity for growth as opposed to something we should avoid at all cost? Coaching your children through failure, in whatever area that may be, will help your children understand that you love them for who they are, not what they do, and that they can draw learning from life experience that is truly transformational.

Unfortunately, many of us have been taught that failure is bad or something that should be avoided altogether. As a result, we avoid taking risks. Our own fear of failure can prevent our children from moving beyond the walls of 'what is' to 'what could be' when we impose our fears upon them.

The key here is learning, so remember, failing at something does not make our children a failure, and this, more than anything, needs to be communicated so our children understand and believe it.

Failure is an Event, Not a Person

Consider the average child's feelings after they have experienced failure. Do they say, "I'm no good at _____." Or, more often say, "I am no good at anything!"

Failure can produce some incredibly powerful feelings within our children and this is where parents can bring a different and healthier perspective to them. We have an opportunity to teach our children that failure is a natural part of life and learning by;

- Communicating clearly and often that failure is a natural part of life and learning.
- Avoiding a negative over-reaction to their failures.
- Consistently showing that our love for them is unconditional and is not based upon how they 'perform.'
- Openly sharing with them about some of our own failures and the value these experiences have brought into our own lives.

During this time of internal conflict within their lives, we can encourage more reflective thinking by our children which can serve to bring proper perspective to them. You could ask something like,

- "I am not sure I understand, how does your failing at _____, make you a failure?"
- "I don't see a failure. What I see is (name positive character qualities you have seen)."
- "There are many things you're good at. Can you name a few?"

In this way, we emphasize that failing at something is simply an event, not something our child is.

I am not suggesting that we ignore or minimize the pain that failure brings. Here we must draw a healthy balance. On one hand, we want to honor them by allowing them the time they need to process the pain, and on the other hand, we must coach them so that they can reflect upon and draw the greatest learning experience from that pain. Coaching by *Supporting Growth* will help us do this more effectively.

Chapter 13

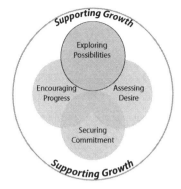

Exploring Possibilities

"Dreaming about my own possibilities was a really neat experience. I got to dream a bit, and then choose something I wanted to do. That was pretty cool."

Chad, 12

Exploring Possibilities turns our child's attention toward the growth opportunity the present situation is offering them and can be as simple as asking,

"What are the possibilities that you see here?"
"What could you do in this situation?"
"What options do you have?"
"What is the best way forward?"

Our focus is upon *Supporting* our child's *Growth* and development, not upon problem solving and offering solutions to them. Every opportunity is an opportunity for growth in some way, so we default to *asking* them to *Explore their Possibilities* and *listening* as they do.

As we begin *Exploring Possibilities*, I would like to contrast the coaching approach of *asking* with the common *telling* approach. When you read the following dialogue between a Dad and his son, observe how the child responds when being told what they should do, and how this influences the conversation between them. Following, contrast that with the response of the child who is asked about his ideas, and notice the difference in how this influences the second conversation.

> **"Our focus is upon *supporting* our child's *growth* and development, not upon problem solving and offering solutions to them."**

Background

Mom and Dad are sitting in the living room together when their son comes home from school and announces that he has a Science Project to do this month.

Telling Approach	Coaching Approach
"Hey, Mom and Dad, I have a Science Project to do this month."	"Hey, Mom and Dad, I have a Science Project to do this month."
"Oh yeah, I remember doing Science Projects in school; they are pretty cool."	*"Oh yeah, I remember doing Science Projects in School; they are pretty cool."*
"Yeah, I guess so."	"Yeah, I guess so."
"I know what you should do."	*"So, have you given it any thought?"*
"Really, what's that?"	"Yeah, a bit."
"Make a volcano!"	*"What do you have in mind so far?"*
"A volcano?"	"Well, I really like the outdoors and stuff like that. Last week, in Science Class we had a man from the Ministry of Natural Resources talking to us. It was pretty cool! All the stuff he gets to do in his job, like canoeing, hiking and giving fines to guys who are doing stuff illegal. He was saying how important biology is and that we need to care for our environment. So, I've been thinking about a couple of things like that."
"Yeah."	
"Why?"	
"Well, when I was in grade 6 I made a volcano, and I can give you a hand with it. It would be easy. See, I made it out of paper mache with a rubber tube running up the center of it. It was attached off the side to a plunger device, and when I pushed the plunger it erupted. It was great, lava flowed up the tube, and spilled over the top and down into the valley below. To top it off, I got a great mark."	
"You know Dad, that sounds cool and all, but ... I don't think so."	*"Sounds interesting. Can I hear them?"*
"Why not?"	"One idea is to test for pollution in water from lakes, rivers and streams around our house, using a bioassay."
"Well, I'm really interested in something else, I had these other two ideas I was considering."	*"A bio – what?"*
"Oh come on. Don't worry about those ideas, this will make it easier on you and I have the experience already. It won't be that difficult, I promise. I can show you everything you need to do to make it work."	"A bioassay, it's a way of testing water by using a living thing, like a vegetable or something like that, then measuring the effect the pollution has on it."
"Honestly Dad, I am not really that interested in making a volcano."	*"That's pretty cool, . . ., I mean, yeah that's what I thought it was."*
"I'm just trying to help you out a bit here. It's your Dad, come on."	"Yeah, right Dad."
"Mom, can you tell Dad that I am not interested? He doesn't seem to be hearing me at all. I'm headin' to my room to veg, call me when supper's ready."	*"You mentioned you had a couple of possibilities, what was the other one?"*
	"Well, the Ministry guy was saying that lots of people are complaining about the Cormorant populations in the area. There are just too many of them and they are eating all the fish. I thought it would be cool to check our lake out and see if there are Cormorant nests and how many there are. Maybe I could figure out how that is affecting our lake here."
	"Those are both great ideas. Have you settled in on one you'd like to do?"

Notice the difference between the conversations above. The *telling approach* focuses upon the parent's agenda without considering what the child desires at all. Dad has assessed the 'situation,' there is a project to be done this month. He then strategized a 'solution,' they'll make a volcano, because that's what he did in Elementary School. Following that, he tried to 'convince' his son to embrace his 'solution.' By doing this he short-circuited a potential growth opportunity for his son and missed a great opportunity for relational connection which *asking* and *listening* would have provided.

On the other hand we see an entirely different outcome with the *coaching approach*. The Father honored his son by *asking* and *listening*. Dad fostered a relational connection which *Supports Relationship* and makes the transition to *Supporting Growth* natural and easy. This approach affirms the value of his son's ideas, making it easier for him to open up and share ideas in the future. After the affirmation, Dad asks if he has settled in on which he would like to do. Dad begins to *Assess Desire* here, and depending on the son's response, he could *Explore* more *Possibilities* or simply *Secure* a *Commitment* to move forward.

Overall, this is a much healthier relational approach that leaves the doors of communication wide open and has a more positive impact upon the relationship than simply offering solutions or telling our children what they should do. It is our job to ensure that our children are doing the thinking here, not do the thinking for them. As their coach, we challenge them to think about their situation and consider all the possibilities.

What Kids are Saying.

How do you feel when your parents ask for your input on and allow you to make decisions, and sometimes even experience some of the painful consequences of those decisions?

"Wow, that's a good question, I don't know how to answer this because I've never experienced it."

Eric, 16

"When my parents began using the coaching approach it felt strange to me. I was used to being told what to do, not asked what I thought about the situation or decision. At first I was hesitant, thinking that they were 'baiting me' and didn't really want to say much. But they continued asking and listening and over time I realized they were genuine and really wanted to help me learn to make decisions and carry greater responsibility on my own. I feel like we have a whole new relationship and my respect for them has grown."

Sierra, 17

Five Options Technique

A useful technique in this stage is the five options technique. When our children are facing a challenge on their own, there is a tendency to stop thinking creatively after two or three options. If these options are not appealing to our children, they tend to become stuck and don't know what to do. The five options technique helps build momentum by challenging our child to think beyond the initial set of options and get back into the creative zone. To do this we can simply ask for five options about how they could move forward with their situation, issue, or concern. Then give them the time they need to generate five options.

If this comes easily to the child, we could simply ask for 7 or 8 options instead.

- "Give me five options for how you can approach this."
- "If there were something we haven't thought of yet in that mind of yours, what would it be?"
- "What's another possibility?"
- "Give me one more."
- "What else could you do?"
- "If you stepped outside of the box, what would you try?"

Be Aware of Our Reactions

Children are very creative, resourceful and have vivid imaginations. What they consider a great possibility may be startling or even seem unrealistic to us. We must pay particular attention to our body language at this time and what it may communicate about their ideas. The rolling of eyes, the words we speak, or sighing in disbelief have the potential to shut our children down if they perceive that their ideas are being judged negatively. Our purpose during this stage is not to evaluate the possibilities; rather, it is to create as many as they can. Afterward they will select one that appeals most to them as they move toward their objective. Remember, every possibility is a good possibility, until they choose the best. By allowing our children to *Explore Possibilities* we open the door to their creativity, and who knows, they may even surprise us by creating an effective course of action we would never have thought of.

Example

One afternoon my 6 year old son was noticeably frustrated with his schoolwork. His body language and attitude spoke loud and clear. I began talking with him about this, to see if he could help me understand what was taking place that caused him to react as he was. To my surprise, he quickly retorted, "I should just quit school and be done with it all." Maintaining my composure, I thought, "let's utilize this as a growth opportunity and see where it goes." I responded, "Yes, Josh, that is one possibility for you to consider. What else do you think you could do?"

"It is our job to ensure that our children are doing the thinking, not do their thinking for them."

His head snapped up, almost startled by my response, then he proceeded to talk about other ways in which he could deal with his frustration. By not reacting to him in this situation and allowing 'quitting school' to be placed on the table as a possibility, honored him and his ability to think through this situation. Simply allowing him to speak, and listen as he did, gave him time to cool off and settle on a more 'reasonable' course of action.

Open Questions that Help Children Explore their Possibilities

- "What are the possibilities here?"
- "How could we move forward with what you want to accomplish?"
- "How could you move forward from here?"
- "What are 5 things you could possibly do?"
- "What else?"
- "What could help you reach your objective?"

Early Beginnings

Coaching can begin very early within our children's development, and doing so, we will quickly recognize the benefit coaching offers to both us and our children. By asking our children to begin thinking on their own, and *Exploring Possibilities* we may notice times in which they are legitimately *stumped*. Remember, our goal is to assist them in their growth and development according to their *Natural Growth Patterns*. It is healthy to think in terms of stepping stones. In moments like these, when our children are legitimately stumped, you may ask the same question that one of our first *Pro-Active Parent Coaching* course attendees did.

> "If my child doesn't seem to have an answer or the ability to dream of possibilities can I offer suggestions to him?"

> Yes, but with guidelines.

1. **Default to coaching first by asking the child to think for themselves.** In this way, we communicate our belief in their ability to think of possibilities. It also helps us ensure that their resources are exhausted before adding ours to the mix. When we recognize that they are truly stuck, then it is appropriate to ask them for permission to make suggestions.
2. **Ask permission to make suggestions.** We could begin by saying something like, "May I offer something else for you to consider?" or "Would you be interested in some ideas I might have?" or "Would it help you if I offered some suggestions here?" Crossing the line and making suggestions when they are not 'interested' in them, or simply do not want us to, only serves to shut our children down and potentially create resentment.
3. **Give them permission to accept or decline our ideas.** Reaffirm that the final choice will be theirs. They have permission to accept or decline our ideas without recourse of any kind.
4. **Always make multiple suggestions.** By doing this our children must still choose between options they will commit to.

For example,

- "You could _____ or _____; which would you prefer?"
- "Would you rather _____ or _____?"
- "You're welcome to _____ or _____."
- "In this situation you could _____ or _____; or, is there something else that comes to mind?"

By asking if there is 'something else', we allow them the freedom to think and add to the options as they are able to.

One cautionary note: we must be prepared and be willing to live with the consequences of the suggestions we provide for our child to choose between. For example, if you live on a busy street, with high traffic you may want to be careful what option you give. "You could play in the back yard or the front yard, (where the greater potential of danger is); either choice is fine." When in reality, either choice is not fine.

> "My parents and I talk a lot, they have become my biggest supporters. Instead of telling me what to do they ask for my input and really guide me in my decision making. There have been times when they have let me make decisions that were bad and did hurt a bit. You know what, I respect them for that, and think if they would have told me not to, I probably would have done it anyway. What hit me the most was, they didn't beat me up by saying, 'I knew it wouldn't work out,' but simply asked me what I learned through the experience and what I'd do differently the next time around. I know that they truly care for me and want what's best."
>
> Daniel, 17

When we have begun *Supporting Growth* through *E.A.S.E.*, we recognize just how creative our children can be at *Exploring Possibilities*. It is not just about solving problems, but about the possibility of growth in every situation. When they have dreamed up as many possibilities as they can, we can then turn our focus upon *Assessing Desire* so that we can *Secure Commitment,* that will be followed through with.

Reflection

Notice the emphasis in *Pro-Active Parent Coaching* is upon helping our children engage with and reflect upon their own situations, then dream of *possibilities* about how they can grow through them.

- What benefit do you see by using this approach?
- In what ways will this impact them personally?
- In what way can this shape their thinking in the future?

Chapter

14

Assessing Desire

The Power of Desire

Assessing Desire is a critical component of coaching prior to *Securing Commitment*. In this stage we are assessing our child's motivation level and which possibility they will be most committed to. This is important to ensure that our child 'owns' the action and is not simply doing it because Mom or Dad think it's a great idea or they are 'being told' to do so.

Prioritizing motivation over information makes an incredible difference in how we approach our children's growth and learning. When we believe that in order for our child to grow, learn or change, we must tell them what they need to do, we will continue to 'do for and tell.' However, when we believe the most important factor is motivation, we will naturally begin coaching and keying in on our child's desire: because we know that the buy-in and motivation is highest for steps children create on their own.

The biggest obstacle to growth and change is motivation, not information. Knowing what to do does not produce change; there has to be a desire for change. This is easily seen in the fact that we know we should eat healthily and exercise to maintain our physical health (information), but often don't do so until a health issue arises and we 'must' change (motivation). In the same way, we may have a great idea about how our child could grow in a specific area, but if they are not motivated to do so, all of our telling (information) will have little effect upon them.

Our children, like us, are most motivated to act on their own ideas and these ideas flow from their desire. Therefore if we want to *Support Growth*, we need to tap into and understand our children's desire, because that is what they will be most willing to commit to.

> **"The biggest obstacle to growth and change is motivation, not information."**
> Tony Stoltzfus

What are they motivated to work on?
How motivated are they?
What do they want to do?

By *Assessing Desire*, we seek to gain an understanding of which possibility our child is most motivated to work on. This will allow us to *Secure Commitment* to the possibility that has the greatest potential of being followed through with.

Most of the time this will be a quick and easy step because:

- The possibilities were already considered to some degree as they talked about them.
- One or two may stick out in their mind as something they would like to pursue further.
- These possibilities are most often their own ideas and that makes them very attractive.
- Our child has been directly involved in the process and this raises interest, motivation and buy in because they are not being 'told' what they could or should do.

In *Assessing Desire*, we simply draw our child's attention back to the possibilities they created and ask something like;

- "As you consider these possibilities, (list them), which appeals to you the most?"
- "You have thought of some great possibilities here; which would you like to pursue?"
- "Out of all of these possibilities, which do you like the best?"
- "What would you like to do?"

Exercise

Take a couple of minutes and write down three questions you could ask your child to help you *Assess* their level of *Desire*.

Your Questions:

-

-

-

Tone and Body Language

During this stage we must pay particular attention to our child's tone and body language. Are they excited? Do they show this in the tone of their voice and their body language? Is there enthusiasm? Our last question, "Is that something you'd like to do?" tests the level of desire they have and naturally gives us permission to *Secure Commitment*.

For instance, in conversation we may ask, *"Is that something you would like to do?"* If they respond, "Yeah, I guess that's an OK idea." What would you think? Do they sound highly motivated? Is there a strong desire to move forward? Will they make a solid commitment?

> "By *Assessing Desire*, we seek to gain an understanding of which possibility our child is most motivated to work on."

Probably not; if we receive a response like this, it may indicate that they would prefer to take another course of action, and as their coach it is better to pursue their desire, than try to force commitment here.

On the other hand, we may ask that same question and if they respond, "Yeah, I'd love to do that, it'd be fun!" We can be certain that we have found something they will commit to.

> **In conversation we are focusing on,**
>
> **Possibilities:** What are the possibilities here?
> **Desire:** What is our child's motivation level?
> **Commitment:** What will they commit to?

Keys to Keeping Motivation High

- **Begin small**. Supporting our children's growth is about helping them grow in their ability, not cutting them loose all at once. So begin small; allowing them to experience success as stepping stones.

- **Set goals that they can meet.** We must always be mindful of the fact that actions too big or too small will drain our children's energy and confidence, impacting their motivation. If the commitment is too big, it may become discouraging; if it is too small, they may become bored and disinterested. The key is balance. A good question to ask is, 'What will encourage just enough action to stretch our children, encourage growth, and at the same time maintain their physical, emotional and spiritual health?'

- **Encourage progress.** Find ways to celebrate and encourage their progress in ways that honor them and that they will appreciate.

- **Talk often.** Taking the time needed to talk openly and often will keep our children's motivation high or give them a boost in motivation if it is needed. Interestingly enough, many people believe that as our children mature, they need less of our time. Actually, the opposite is true. As our children mature, we need to focus more time on supporting them with healthy conversation.

Assessing Desire is critical, it gives us a greater understanding of what our child is motivated and energized to work on. This makes our transition to Securing Commitment more natural and effective, and their commitment more meaningful and significant.

> ## Reflection
> - Why would it be important to *Assess Desire* before asking for a commitment?
> - What does this step in the process do for us as parents?
> - In what ways do I see this benefiting my child's ability to make commitment?
> - How could this help in my own parenting?

Chapter 15

15

Securing Commitment

> "Unless commitment is made, there are only promises and hopes... but no plans."
> Peter Drucker

There is a difference between interest and commitment. When you're interested in something you do it when it's convenient. When you're committed to something, you make sure it gets done.

"Commitment goes beyond making a choice. Every day we make choices such as how we dress in the morning; casual or formal, what we eat for breakfast; eggs or waffles. However, commitments are solid and carry greater weight, such as our commitment to God; to one another; or to a course of action."[5]

Commitment speaks of priority, "I will do this!" and is essential for providing healthy accountability and encouraging our child's progress. It is here that we draw a line in the proverbial sandbox and ask our children to come across onto our side by *Securing a Commitment* to action. This act challenges them to move beyond simply dreaming and talking, to doing.

> "Will you do that?"
> "Will you commit to that plan of action?"

When our child says, "Yes, I will commit to that," this is a powerful act for both us and them. It raises the probability of follow through, and provides us with the opportunity to offer healthy accountability as they move toward their objectives.

> "Dad, are you trying to help me be a better decision maker?" my inquisitive son's eyes peered across the boat cover as we snapped it back into place.
> *Looking over at him and smiling I responded, "What makes you ask that, Josh?"*

"Well, it's just every time I am making a decision, you won't tell me what to do, but you ask me to choose and what will I commit to. So I got thinking, you must be trying to help me be a better decision maker. Are you?"

"You're very observant, Josh. As a matter of fact, I am. Would you like to know why?"

"Yeah, that'd be great, Dad."

Leaning upon the boat I looked across into his eyes, and began, *"Well, Josh, all throughout your life you will be faced with decisions, many small ones and some really big ones."*

"Like who I will marry when I get older, right!?"

Laughing,I replied, *"Yes, that is one of the big decisions you will face in life. But before you face that one, which is many, many years away, Mommy and Daddy simply want to help you become the best decision maker you can be. That way, when you are older, you will have experience making decisions, but also committing to and following through with them. You know, you're a very smart young man for picking up on the fact we are trying to help you like this."*

"Thanks, Dad."

When we call our children to commitment, there is no doubt that within the hearts and minds of our children there is a mental shift taking place, similar to Joshua's above. There is a realization, "Hey, we're not just talking about possibilities here, we're talking about a commitment! This is 'grown up' stuff."

Moving from Desire to Securing a Commitment to Action

After *Assessing Desire, Securing Commitment* can be as simple as asking,

> "In light of all of this, what will you do, and by when?"

This question intentionally shifts our child's attention from the possibilities, through what they would like to do, to what they will do.

"Commitment speaks of priority, 'I will do this!'" It is an important step because we can talk about a lot of good things to do, create some great possibilities, and even say, "That's a great idea, I'd like to do that sometime." But, without Securing a Commitment, 'sometime' rarely happens.

The value of *Securing Commitment* is seen in the fact that it establishes a course of action; what will be done, and the time frame within which it will happen. This makes accountability possible, but also provides very clear expectations between us and our children. We know exactly what they intend to do, and this alleviates unnecessary relational conflict due to misunderstandings or unclear/un-met expectations. We never conclude this stage of our coaching conversation before *Securing Commitment* by asking our child to verbalize exactly what they will do and by when.

> What will you do, by when?
> How will you know this is accomplished?
> How will I know?

> **3 Tests of an Action Step**
> **Clarity**: Both we, and our child will know exactly what will be done.
> **Commitment**: Our child has taken responsibility and will do this.
> **Conclusion**: There is a specific time line established.

It is very important that we establish a way to remember what *commitment* they are making, so that we can re-engage conversation and begin *Encouraging* their *Progress*. As our children mature, they can begin tracking their own commitments on a calendar of some sort which will help them learn valuable time management principles.

Giving Permission to Re-adjust their Commitment

Every once in a while as we walk through this process we may notice that there seems to be a lack of ownership to the commitment they are making, or indecision on the child's part. In other words, the process has broken down somewhere along the way, or they are wanting to re-adjust their commitments.

When we discover this, we simply need to step back, giving our children permission to 'change their mind,' and revisit *E.A.S.E.* For an example of this you can take another look at Katelyn's story, when I had given her permission to change her mind about a decision she was making. It is found in Chapter 5 with the conversation beginning on page 65.

> **"Commitment makes accountability possible, but also provides very clear expectations between us and our children."**

In these moments we can use one of the following questions which will help our children reconnect with their desire or bring clarity to the commitment they are making.

- "It seems as though you may not be really excited about that step. Remember, you have permission to change your mind. Is there something else you'd rather do?"
- "Is there another approach you'd rather take? If so, let's talk about that."
- "Are you ready to commit to that?"
- "You mentioned that you might do_____; is there anything keeping you from saying, I will do _____?"
- "You are saying you 'ought to do this.' What would make that into something you would really want to do?"
- "This is entirely up to you; it's your choice. You can do it or not do it; what will you choose?"
- "Is there anything else on your mind that you'd like to talk about before you make a solid commitment to this? If so, what is it?"

Securing Commitment is essential to supporting our children's growth and providing the necessary encouragement and accountability they will need as they strive toward their growth objectives. Once our child has verbalized their commitment, we are well positioned to *Encourage* their *Progress*.

Reflection

- What is the importance of asking our children what they desire before asking for commitment?
- What is the purpose of following the process completely through to commitment, as opposed to simply asking what they might want or desire?
- What is accomplished by asking our child what they are committing to, as opposed to simply asking what they want to do?
- How could *Securing Commitment* increase our child's ability to follow through?

Chapter 16

Encouraging Progress

> "My parents are very encouraging; they help me to make my own decisions, and follow-up with me to see how I am doing. When I do something well, they push me to grow more, and when I come up short, they support me by talking openly about it. It is neat how they can point out things in my life I am doing well, even when I feel like a failure. I like it when they do that."
>
> Theo, 12

Nothing builds our children's morale more than having them commit to a course of action and then offering them the support they need to accomplish it. The nature of growth in any area of life is such that there needs to be commitment and self-reflection throughout the process. *Encouraging Progress* provides our children with a healthy accountability structure, an opportunity to reflect upon their experience, and the encouragement they need to keep moving forward.

Our children cannot be supported from a distance or by short bursts of attention. They need time, planned time, not just a few words and a pat on the back as we walk out the door. The great news for our children is that as we put *Pro-Active Parent Coaching* into practice, we are well on the way to offering this kind of support. Taking the time to talk with our children about their progress communicates that we truly love them, we care about them, we believe in them, and we support them throughout their learning process.

> **"Encouragement is oxygen to the soul."**
> George Adams

There are four fundamental elements within *Encouraging Progress*: *Celebrating Progress, Expressing Belief, Acknowledgement,* and providing *Healthy Accountability*. All of which are supported by the power of our words, so let's turn our attention to the power of our words for a moment.

The Power of Words

Words have a powerful impact. Solomon wisely said, "The tongue has the power of life and death." (Proverbs 18:21) We have the ability to bring life to and energize our children, but we also have the power to discourage, and it largely depends upon the spirit of our words. What is our intention when talking to them, to bring life and to build them up, or, something else?

> **"The tongue has the power of life and death."**
> Proverbs 18:21
> (NIV)

The old mantra, "Sticks and stones may break my bones but your words will never hurt me," couldn't be further from the truth. It would be better stated, "Sticks and stones may break my bones and your words will always shape me," because our words have a powerful influence upon our children. Our words shape their perceptions of and belief about themselves and impact their overall wellbeing.

Exercise

Moving from Criticism to Praise

Spend time with your child and tune into your own thoughts. As you interact with your child, take note of what critical thoughts surface. Now take a moment to refocus, and intentionally think of something that you appreciate about them.

- What do you most appreciate about your child?
- How have they added value to your life?
- In what ways do they enrich you?

If you have been practicing the previous coaching skills, this will be a relatively easy exercise for you. For some, though, this will be a stretch. Remember, the quality of your relationship together will be largely determined by how you perceive your child and communicate with them. This is largely an issue of the heart, Jesus said, "Out of the abundance of the heart, the mouth speaks." (Luke 6:45) Our words truly reveal what is contained within our hearts about our children.

Our children need and value constructive feedback; we all do. Encouragement truly is oxygen to the soul, and because of this, Pro-Active Parent Coaches choose to intentionally relate to our children in terms of who they are becoming, not in terms of what they are lacking.

> **"Our children need and value constructive feedback, we all do."**

It is interesting to me that God does the same thing with us as His children. He relates to us in terms of our destiny, as opposed to all that we lack. A quick look at Ephesians 2 reveals His character and approach to us. Although we were dead in trespasses and sin, He chose us; what's more is, He provided the means of reconciliation with Himself through the sacrifice of Jesus Christ. He says, 'I know your destiny, I know the potential that resides within you, and I will support your growth toward its fulfillment'.

The support we give our children through positive feedback provides them with a healthy perspective, gives a sense of purpose to what they are doing, and an energy boost to continue moving forward.

Reflection

Take a few moments and think about a time that you were recognized and celebrated.
- "How did that make you feel?"
- "How did it affect the rest of your day?"
- "How did it affect your relationship with the people who honored you?"

Celebrating Progress

It is easy for anyone to become discouraged, to lose focus and the motivation to continue moving forward. There are times that the distance between where we are and the goal we have set seems so overwhelming that it overshadows the progress we have already made. Our perspective becomes lost and our motivation decreases, and, sometimes, the will to continue just isn't there!

Thinking about this for a moment may bring another realization to the surface. If I, as an adult, can sometimes lose perspective in this way, how much easier would it be for my child to do so?

> **"It is easy for anyone to become discouraged, to lose focus and the motivation to continue moving forward."**

It's in moments like these, when someone comes alongside of us with an encouraging word, to challenge us and help us regain perspective, that we often discover a renewed energy and enthusiasm to push forward. As parent coaches, we have a prime opportunity to renew our children's perspective and give them the energy they need to continue through *Celebrating Progress*.

On any given day we may notice that our child has lost focus, or has grown discouraged in some way with the progress they are making. Focussing on and celebrating the progress they have already made could be the 'oxygen' they need in the moment.

Taking the time to tell them what we see, the steps forward they are making, the growth they have shown, and/or the accomplishments they have already attained is a powerful motivator and helps them regain a healthy perspective on the larger picture.

If we want to help them gain perspective we could ask a variation of the following:

- "I see what you have accomplished already; can *you* tell me what you've accomplished?"
- "I know you may not have reached your goal yet, but can you tell me how far you have already come?"
- "It looks as if you've worked very hard on that; how do you think you did?"

Expressing Belief

Have you ever had someone tell you that they believed in you, when you didn't even believe in yourself? How did that influence your thinking? Did it give you the internal strength to move forward in an area you otherwise may have given up on or not tried at all?

As a parent coach we bring power and energy to our children's dreams and desires when we honor, hold onto and believe in them. We express belief when we remind them of what they are aiming for and affirm,

"I believe in you!"
"I know you can do it."

> **"We bring power and energy to our children's dreams and desires when we honor, hold onto, and believe in them."**

I remember a conversation that our second daughter, Hannah, initiated by asking, "Dad, do you think I am responsible enough to baby sit?" What motivated such a question? She had a belief within herself that she may be responsible enough and quite honestly wanted to know if Dad believed the same about her. Expressing our belief is a powerful motivator for our children, causing them to rise to the occasion and reach for our expectations. What was my response? *"Yes, honey, I do. You have shown yourself to be responsible in many areas, and I have no doubt in my mind, that you are responsible enough to baby sit. As a matter of fact, I'd trust you to care for Joshua."* That expression of belief gave her the strength and confidence she needed from us as parents, and shortly thereafter she enrolled in a baby sitting course and received her license.

Expressing Belief can happen anytime and anywhere. For example, this past summer Joshua took a strong interest in skate boarding. Having visited a yard sale he saw a used skateboard for $5.00. He purchased the board and a set of elbow, knee and wrist guards for an additional $10.00. Armed with his new gear and the helmet we previously purchased for Josh, he was set to go. He spent hours practicing, getting used to the board and, of course, picking himself up off the pavement, but with time and practice he became quite proficient at skating.

On our 'date' days, we would go to the skateboard park and play around, and watch the 'pros,' as he called them, do their tricks.

Then it happened. On one blistering hot afternoon, two months later, Joshua climbed to the top of a 'half pipe,' placed his skateboard on the rail and stood poised peering over the drop off. "Dad, I'm a bit scared," he said, "but I so badly want to try it." *"I think I can understand both your fear and desire."* I replied, *"You're welcome to try it, or wait until another day; either choice is fine."* "But I really want to try today! Do you really think I can do this?" he asked, as his brown eyes peered out below the ridge of his helmet. *"Josh,"* I replied, *"from what I have seen of you and your commitment to learning to skate, I am sure you will master the half pipe. It may not happen on your first or even second try, but you know as well as I, falling is a part of learning. But, yes, I believe you can do it."*

After a few moments of reflection, he leaned forward shifting his weight on the skateboard and began his drop over the edge. Before either one of us knew what was happening, he was lying flat on his stomach, arms beside him, groaning, "Oh that hurts, but it was so cool." He tried, and tried again, but didn't master the half pipe that afternoon. Josh was sore and slightly bruised as we travelled home, and Mom and Dad simply encouraged him to remember, *"The only way to learn is to get a few scrapes and bruises along the way."*

The next morning, he awoke with a new and almost contagious enthusiasm and said, "Mom, Dad, I think I know what I was doing wrong, it was the way I was holding my weight over the board. Can we go back and try again today?" We obliged, and much to our surprise within a couple of tries he was successfully navigating the 'half pipe.'

On the one hand, these simple expressions of belief brought a sense of responsibility and boosted Hannah's confidence, and on the other, gave Joshua courage as he faced the prospect of pain and did something he may otherwise not have tried until much later.

> **"Simple expressions of belief encourage responsibility and boost our children's confidence."**

Exercise

Expressing Belief is communicating what we believe our child is capable of. Take a few moments and think through the follow questions.

- What is one thing about my child in which I can express belief to them?
- What positive thing do I believe about my child's future, based on what I have seen so far?
- What skills, habits and abilities does my child have, that I see leading them to future success?
- What are they truly capable of in life?
- What potential is present that I can draw out by expressing my belief in them?

At the next opportunity, take time to express belief in your son or daughter and pay particular attention to how that influences their level of confidence.

Acknowledgement

Encouraging Progress is all about supporting our children's growth, but growth is so much more than simply what they do or accomplish. Reaching their objective is important, but pales in comparison to who they are becoming while they reach for their objective.

Although praise and compliments are important, they tend to focus primarily upon what our children do, highlighting what they have accomplished. Acknowledgement on the other hand, affirms who they are becoming and speaks to the character God is forming within them. Notice the difference between, "You did a great job cutting the lawn yesterday!" and, "You are becoming a very responsible young man or woman." The compliment goes to their head, while the acknowledgement settles in their heart.

The fact is that when we acknowledge the inner character qualities of our child, it goes right to their core to inspire, motivate and energize them. It brings a character quality to light giving them an opportunity to explore, examine and consider it in greater detail, when it might have been missed or otherwise overlooked.

Reflection

Everyone appreciates a sincere acknowledgment. Think back on the last time someone gave you a real honest to goodness, heartfelt acknowledgment. Not a compliment, or praise for a job well done, but an authentic observation about who you were in that moment.

- "You showed great integrity with that decision!"
- "You left it all on the field; your commitment to the team is incredible!"
- "It's easy to see that you value family, and that will make a difference in your child's life!"

A well placed acknowledgment can, quite frankly, make your day! So take a moment and recall a time you received such an acknowledgement and answer the following questions.

- What thoughts went through your mind when you received that acknowledgement?
- How did that influence your thinking about yourself?
- How did that influence your thinking about the one who acknowledged you?
- What difference did that make within your life?

"A sincere acknowledgement helps our child see themselves as God sees them."

We do not have to look any further than Jesus' conversation with Simon Peter to recognize this principle in action. In speaking with Simon, Jesus could have focussed on many things: what he did or didn't accomplish, his shortcomings, that he would one day be a great speaker, communicator, evangelist and church planter. Instead, Jesus saw something much more important than what he would accomplish. Jesus recognized, then verbalized a character quality that was deep inside of Simon. "You are Simon son of John, but you will be called Peter," which means, 'You are a rock!' (See John 1:42)

Jesus' focus was upon Simon's character; who he was, as opposed to what he was doing. I wonder what he thought when he heard these words from Jesus. "Who me? You've got to be kidding, I am the furthest thing from a rock. I am not sure who you're looking at, Jesus, but it can't be me!" Or, "Wow, you really see that in me Jesus?" "Jesus, those words stir something within me, there is just something about what you said, and I really want to live up to that!"

Acknowledgement goes right to our child's heart, and affirms who they are as a person. It allows them to take notice of something deeper within them, may cause them to stand a little taller, and desire to fulfill what we see within them.

Exercise

Acknowledgement affirms who our children are deep down inside. Take a few moments and think about the following questions:
- What character qualities do I admire within my child?
- What is their true value?
- What inner greatness and potential do I see?
- What is the hidden treasure inside them that they may not see?
- What does God see within them that He wants me to draw out?

There are three parts to a powerful *acknowledgment*. The first is to actually recognize the character quality and verbalize it; the second is to allow time for our child to receive it and feel it's impact; the third is, speak it with sincerity. In light of this, take your observation from the exercise above and formulate an acknowledgment that you can give your child in the space provided below. Afterwards, take the next opportunity to acknowledge your child and watch how they respond.

> **"Acknowledgement goes right to our child's heart, and affirms who they are as a person."**

Acknowledgement

A sincere *acknowledgement* helps our child see themselves as God sees them and who knows, they may even think to themselves, "Mom, Dad, those words stir something within me, there is just something about what you said, and I really want to live up to that!"

We Must Ask to Provide Support

Only in asking about our child's progress can we provide the necessary support, encouragement and accountability our children need for their growth and development. If there is no accountability, it is very easy to put things off or let other circumstances get in the way of accomplishing our objectives. It is amazing how much more someone can accomplish when they know they will be asked about it. This is a simple but powerful relational principle that *Supports Growth* and can easily be applied within our parenting.

> **"Our focus is upon *Supporting Growth.* Therefore, we intentionally take a positive view and consciously choose to focus upon progress made."**

The final element of *Encouraging Progress* is the accountability conversation. This conversation infuses life into our children through continued support as they move toward their objectives. It is within the context of conversation that we *Celebrate Progress, Express Belief* and sincerely *Acknowledge* our children. In a way, the accountability conversation is like a revolving door; it will take us to our desired destination, but also bring us back to the starting point again, providing a healthy, and continued support structure for our children.

As we prepare to ask the accountability question, our focus is upon *Supporting Growth. Therefore,* we intentionally take a positive view and consciously choose to focus upon *progress* made, as opposed to what is lacking.

Observe the Difference Between the Following

"Remember when we talked about _____. Did you do it?"

Contrast that with asking a question something like this:

"Hey, kiddo, give me a quick update on what you have accomplished with _____."

The differences are subtle, but the implications can be strong.

"Did you do it?" Is very specific and we will receive either a yes or no answer, but it carries with it an attitude that can be interpreted as, "You probably didn't do it." "There is probably something wrong." "I didn't believe you would." Questions that carry the possibility of being interpreted in this way can turn our children off of accountability and create the thoughts or feelings of, "Why should I even bother; you never believe I can do it anyway?" "Why try? Nothing I do is ever good enough for you!"

"Give me an update on what you have accomplished?" or "Tell me about your progress," are much more positive and expresses belief that the child has indeed made progress. Further, it will be noticed and celebrated no matter how big or small the step is. This creates within our children a sense of satisfaction and accomplishment, providing them with the necessary emotional energy they need to continue moving toward their objectives.

Reflection

In order to support our child's growth we must ask about their progress. There are three simple keys in asking. a. We ask a direct question. b. We ask in a positive manner. c. Our focus is upon *Encouraging Progress*, not highlighting what is lacking. Consider the following questions.

- What would happen if we didn't ask about our children's progress with their action steps and simply let it go?
- What are the benefits of asking about our children's progress?

Take a few moments and write down two accountability questions you could ask your child that would focus upon what they have accomplished, as opposed to their shortcomings.

- "When we talked last week, you made a commitment to speak with your teacher about your public presentation. Give me an update on that." (Specific and assumes action was taken)

-

-

Healthy Accountability

Many of us have shied away from *accountable relationships* over the years simply because we have had bad experiences with them. What we expected to give us encouragement and the energy we needed to sustain change or growth within our lives actually did the opposite. It left us feeling condemned, defeated and/or discouraged.

Healthy accountability energizes and motivates our children as opposed to leaving them with the feeling of being watched over and controlled. Accountability within the coaching relationship is not delivering punishment for wrong behavior, or making our children feel ashamed and guilty when they blow it. It isn't about judging, blaming or scolding at all. In fact, *healthy accountability* focuses and builds upon our children's progress, providing the necessary feedback and encouragement that will serve to strengthen their desire to continue moving forward.

It is simply a means by which our children can communicate their progress on what they have committed to, and alter their course as necessary. In this way, healthy accountability is not about us as parents at all. Remember, coaching involves understanding where our child is, knowing where they want to go, and giving them the support they need to get there.

Accountability that is firm but gentle energizes and encourages our children, while at the same time continues to foster health within our relationship together. It is here we see strength within the interdependent relationship. On the other hand, if we try to motivate our children through fear, shame or guilt, they will withdraw from us and seek the encouragement they need elsewhere.

Unhealthy Accountability vs. Healthy Accountability

I'd like to illustrate the difference between unhealthy and *healthy accountability* as we bring *Encouraging Progress* to a conclusion. We will observe two conversations. The first illustrates unhealthy accountability and shows how we can discourage our children.

The second demonstrates how *healthy accountability Encourages Progress*. This serves to strengthen relationship but also provides our children with the emotional energy they need to continue moving toward their objectives.

Background

In the following conversation, this young man indicated that he wanted to improve his marks in school and gave his Dad permission to coach him through this growth issue. After *Exploring Possibilities* and *Assessing Desire*, he *Secured Commitment* to increase his study time at home by one hour each school day, beginning immediately.

The commitment is clear and concise which allows for accountability because both the young man and Dad know exactly what the action step is.

> **"Accountability is *NOT* delivering punishment for wrong behavior, or making our children feel ashamed and guilty when they blow it."**

Example 1 Unhealthy Accountability

Observe the following conversation and notice how Dad holds his son accountable. Think about what might be happening within the mind of this child.

- Will he be motivated to continue moving toward his goal?
- What would you expect this to do within the parent/child relationship?
- Lastly, will the son want to continue this accountability relationship?

Unhealthy Accountability Conversation	Observation
"So when we last talked about your homework, you said you wanted to do better. How is that going for you?" "Well, it's been fine, I mean, homework is homework, right? But, yeah, I've been doing OK." *"So have you been having any difficulties with it?"* "Umm...no, it's been OK, I mean it could always be better; some subjects I have more difficulty with than others, but overall it's been OK." *"So how many evenings did you actually spend the 1 hour doing homework?"*	This is too general of a question for *healthy accountability* and truly understanding what has been accomplished. No information on the boy's progress has been given, so Dad asks again but with a negative focus on difficulties. The parent now tries to get the information he requires by restating the original goal in question form.

"Umm...well, I did 2 or 3 times each week."

"So your goal was to do it every evening, and there are 5 evenings in the school week; you said you did 2 or 3. Can you tell me how many you actually missed, was it 2 or 3?"

"Yeah, well, it was 3."

"OK, so you missed 3 evenings, which is actually more than you did! How do you expect to reach your goal if you can't even hit the 50% mark the first month you've been doing this?"

"But Dad, I mean . . . . it's been hard. I have all of these respon . . ."

"Come on, son, think about it, 50% is barely a pass, and you didn't come close to accomplishing your objective. If you want to be successful in life, realize now that this is just one step in the process. What will it take for you to meet your goals?"

"Dad, come on, it's just homework, I am not failing at it or anything; I just wanted to improve my overall marks a bit, that's all. Don't get so stressed out!"

"You know what? I am beginning to think you were not serious about this whole thing anyway. I don't know why I try to help you. You say you're going to do something and you don't follow through. This is just a waste of my time and yours."

"You know what Dad? You always go off on me like this! I am not sure what I could ever do to please you. Nothing is ever good enough for you!"

The focus here is upon what the child 'failed' to accomplish.

Dad emphasizes how much was missed, and proceeds to ask a derogatory question.

Dad has failed to *connect, ask and listen* so that he can understand what is really happening here. He is now cutting his son off and beginning to lecture.

Conversation has degraded into accusation which simply serves to drive a wedge relationally between both father and son.

Reflection

- What would a conversation like this do within the parent/child relationship?
- Does it encourage the child's progress and strengthen their desire to move forward?
- What statements in the conversation drew you to this conclusion?
- Do you think the child would want to continue with this accountability relationship?
- What brings you to that conclusion?

Example 2 Healthy Accountability

Observe the following coaching conversation and notice the difference in how Dad approaches accountability here.

- What do you perceive taking place within their relationship?
- What makes you say this?
- How does Dad encourage his sons' progress while keeping him focused upon the overall goal?
- What strengths do you see in this accountability relationship?

Healthy Accountability Conversation	Observation
"When we last talked about your homework, you set a goal to do an hour of homework per school evening. How are you progressing with that?" "It's been pretty good, I have done it 2 or 3 times each week." *"That sounds good. Which is it, two or three?"* "Well, honestly, it was only two." *"Well, when you think about that, that's two more than you were doing a month ago. You're already making progress, and you're goal is closer than it was. How does it make you feel, knowing you're moving forward in this area?"* "Actually Dad, I feel pretty good about it. Like you said, it is more than I was doing a month ago, and I think I can see the benefit of it already. I still have a way to go, but I'm making strides forward and I can be proud of that." *"Great stuff. So, let's consider your overall progress toward your goal. You are now consistently doing homework for one hour two days per week. What would it take to bump that up to four days as you move toward your goal of five?"* "You know, I've been thinking about this a little bit myself. I would have to bounce some things around a bit to make sure I get the hour done. Like I have basketball practice two times a week and those were two of the days I missed. On those days I could do it during my spare at school when I have no class scheduled or, I could do it right when I get home from school instead of waiting until after practice when I am usually too tired to do it." *"It sounds like you're really on top of this; those are both great possibilities! Is there anything else*	Very specific and draws the child's attention directly to his goal and asks about his progress with it. Direct and positive from the outset. Affirms that any progress is positive and good. Then *clarifies* to ensure he understands exactly what progress has been made. Dad realizes he is 3 days from his goal, but chooses to focus upon what has already been accomplished. He states this and asks his son to reflect upon his feelings about the progress he has made to this point. This brings an encouraging perspective, his son is making progress and this can be celebrated. Dad shows grace by acknowledging his son's small steps forward and not demanding completion all at once. At the same time he focuses his sons' attention on the original goal and asks what steps he could take toward that. Notice he allows this to take place in increments, as opposed to asking him to reach for five, he asks for four. By *asking* and *listening* the conversation opens up and reveals that his son has already been thinking about this. This gives the Dad an opportunity to affirm his son, and *explore* further *possibilities*.

you can think of?"

"Well, I don't like the idea of doing homework on Friday nights. I'd rather be free to relax and just hang out with my friends after the week of school. It's just a thought, but I could bump my Friday night study to Sunday night instead."

"That's a good thought. Is there anything else?"

"Um, I could double up my time one or two nights a week. Instead of doing one hour of study on those nights, try to do two."

"Yup, that's another possibility. Anything else come to mind?"

Dad allows his son to *Explore Possibilities* until he has exhausted all of his ideas.

"No, not really."

"Alright then, these are great ideas and I really think you have a handle on this. Tell me as you think of these four options; doing your work during your spare; doing it right when you get home from school on practice days; Sunday evenings; or doubling up study time some of the nights, which appeals to you the most?"

Dad affirms his son's thoughts and turns to *Assessing his son's Desire.*

Assessing Desire. As the son continues moving toward his goal, Dad wants to ensure he *Secures a Commitment* to what his son is most motivated to work on.

"To be honest, I'd really like to keep my spare open. That way I can hang out with my friends who also don't have classes at that time. Sunday nights we often do things as a family, so I am not sure I want to sacrifice that, and doubling up my study time, well, I don't really care for that either. So I think I would lean more towards doing it right when I get home on days I have practice."

This step is revealing. As Dad listens his son evaluates the possibilities and Dad learns which possibility appeals most to his son. This allows Dad to zero in on and *Secure a Commitment* to what his son will be most motivated to try.

"Is that what you would like to do?"

"Yes."

"That sounds great! So tell me what you're going to do over the next week as you move toward your goal?"

Dad *Secures Commitment* and asks his son to state specifically what he is going to do.

"I will continue what I am doing with my homework in other areas, but on practice days I will do my homework right when I get home from school to make sure it gets done."

"That's great son! I appreciate your dedication and commitment to improving your schoolwork in this way. Would you like me to continue holding you accountable in this area?"

Asking for follow-up which will allow Dad to support his son's growth through *Encouraging* his *Progress.*

"Yes, please do. You can ask me again next week?"

"Count on it! I love seeing your progress; I think it excites me as much as it does you!"

Evaluating the Two Approaches

The Dad in the first story chose to focus upon everything that was wrong. The goal was not met and Dad didn't show grace in this situation. It seems as though Dad began to take responsibility himself for the goal and attempted to use guilt to gain compliance. This only served to drive his son away and discourage him from moving forward. The conversation went downhill fast and resulted in both Dad and son becoming sarcastic and saying things that would hurt one another. Unfortunately, it will take some time and intentional effort to restore this relationship to health and open the son up to an accountability relationship with his father once again. As parents we hold the balance in our hands. We can choose to support and encourage their growth, or we can revert to telling and demanding change. How our children respond depends largely upon how we approach them.

"Healthy accountability energizes and motivates our children as opposed to leaving them with the feeling of being watched over and controlled."

The Dad in the second conversation maintains a focus upon his child's growth, and asks a very specific follow up question. It is direct, to the point and effectively allows him to gain an understanding of where his son is at with the objective he set out to meet. Dad also focuses upon the positive by speaking in terms of progress, indicating an expectation that growth has taken place. Although it comes out that his son didn't even make the 'half way' point, Dad chooses to recognize and celebrate this as a step in the right direction and further, asks his son to consider that himself.

It's a good picture about how we can show grace, but still uphold the standard. The Dad accepts partial progress as a step in the right direction, but also upholds the standard by reaffirming what the original objective is and having his son consider now how he can continue moving toward the goal. Our focus as parent coaches remains upon the bigger picture, which helps us recognize the small steps our children make in growth. They do not have to reach their objectives the first time around. As a matter of fact, growth is often characterized by time and commitment over the long haul, not immediate results.

Overall, the son is encouraged on his growth journey which is characterized by his renewed commitment to continue moving forward. Dad, because of the way in which he provides support and encouragement to his son, is invited along for the journey as well, and there really is no greater privilege for a parent to have.

Reflection

- As you consider offering a *healthy accountability* structure to your child, what benefits do you see this adding to your child's growth?
- In what area(s) of growth can you ask your child the accountability question?

When evaluating the accountability you give your children, there are two simple questions that you can ask yourself to help you determine whether, or not, you are providing healthy accountability.

a. Does it energize them toward fulfilling their objective?
b. Do they want to continue with it?

- How would you and your child respond to these questions today?
- What would it take to move toward a healthy approach to accountability?
- What will you do?

Encouraging Progress involves understanding where our child is, knowing where they want to go, and giving them the support they need to get there. It will provide our children with the necessary support, encouragement and accountability they need for healthy growth and movement toward their objectives. As parent coaches who employ this process, we will create an environment that empowers our children and helps them realize their dreams. Further, we will foster a supportive relationship through which we will maintain a connection and enjoy not only a rich relationship with our child, but the excitement that comes by seeing them grow in responsibility.

> **"Our chief want in life is someone who will inspire us to be what we know we could be."**
> Ralph Waldo Emerson

Conclusion

A Few Final Words

Pro-Active Parent Coaching: Capturing the Heart of Your Child is about responsibility and change. Interestingly enough, as much as the focus is upon our children's growth and change, the primary responsibility in all of this, lies with us as parents. It's really about our taking responsibility and changing how we approach and interact with our children in a way that best serves their growth. In doing so, it supports relationship and growth (change) within our children's lives. As you continue practicing the heart, disciplines and skills of *Pro-Active Parent Coaching* you will naturally transition from 'doing coaching' to 'becoming a coach' and empowering your children in this way will become second nature.

It is my deep conviction that the best coaches for children are their own parents. That means you and I; we are the best coaches for the children God has entrusted to our care. God has given us an incredible privilege of investing in and preparing our children for life, and no one else is in a better position to do so. We have the time, the opportunity, the knowledge of who they are and who they are becoming, to offer them a *Supportive Relationship through Understanding* and *Support their Growth* for the future. It is a high calling, a noble mission, a great cause. It is one that is worth investing in because we are not just raising children, we are raising children raisers and that can influence generations to come. As you journey into *Pro-Active Parent Coaching*, may God bless you with rich, healthy relationships that will last a lifetime.

Pro-Active Parent Coaching Model

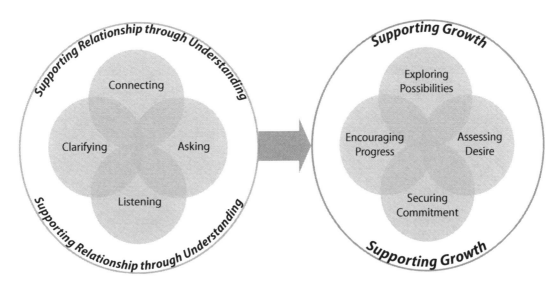

Notes:

1. Angus J. MacQueen. *Producing too Many Squashes*. Online posting. Sermon illustrations. 8 Nov. 2010 <http://bible.org/illustration/producing-too-many-squashes>

2. Carol Carter, Gary Izumo, and Joe Martin. Stop Parenting & Start Coaching (LifeBound, 2004), pp. xvff.

3. Carl R. Rogers. *On Becoming a Person* (Boston: Houghton Mifflin, 1961), pp. 18ff.

4. "understand." Merriam-Webster Online Dictionary. 2008. http://www.merriam-webster.com (3 Nov 2009).

5. Laura Whitworth, Karen Kimsey-House, Henry Kimsey-House, and Phillip Sandahl. *Co-Active Coaching* (Mountainview: Davies-Black Publishing, 2007), pp.148.

Dear Reader

Our family trusts that you have found *Pro-Active Parent Coaching: Capturing the Heart of Your Child* both challenging and rewarding. As you journey into *Pro-Active Parent Coaching yourself*, we'd love to hear about your experience. Please feel free to visit www.pro-activeparentcoaching.com and submit your story to us.

We'd also love your feedback on the book itself. This will help us as we continue producing Parent Coaching resources that are beneficial to people like yourself.

If you would take a few minutes and answer the following questions, we would greatly appreciate it.

1. What impacted me the most?
2. What did I find the most valuable?
3. What other parenting topics would I like help with?
4. What commitment(s) have I made as a result of interacting with this book?
5. Other comments or feedback.

Please feel free to offer your feedback by visiting www.pro-activeparentcoaching.com and selecting the *feedback* option, or, on our Facebook® page, *Pro-Active Parent Coaching: Capturing the Heart of Your Child*. When you do so, please let us know if we have permission to use your feedback in promotional materials for *Pro-Active Parent Coaching*, and/or future parenting resources.

To continue learning and growing in your *Pro-Active Parent Coaching* skills, consider taking one of our tele-classes and enjoy any of the other resources available on our website.

Thank you for your time and consideration with this. Enjoy your journey into *Pro-Active Parent Coaching and the rich relationship you can experience with your children.*

Your friend and pro-active parent coach,

Greg

Made in the USA
San Bernardino, CA
05 July 2016